ARROWMAKER

By

Daniel Hance Page

This book is a work of fiction.
Places, events, and situations in
this story are purely fictional.
Any resemblance to actual persons,
living or dead, is coincidental.

ISBN: 1-4140-0446-X (e-book)
ISBN: 1-4140-0447-8 (Paperback)

This book is printed on acid free
paper.

1stBooks - rev. 10/31/03

"I have traveled a good deal in
Concord."

Henry David Thoreau

FOR

the people who have learned to enjoy the forest and other places of wilderness without harming them.

ONE

<u>THE HUNTER</u>

8000 B.C.

When Skeen circled back to his old trail, he made the chilling discovery that he was being hunted by the hump-backed, grizzly bear. In soft earth, by the water's edge, Skeen saw his own footprints. Upon some of these prints, there were tracks of the great bear. Skeen checked more prints in an attempt to dispel his worries; however his concern increased as he continued to see his old footprints being bordered, or covered, by the large, bear tracks.

With the realization he was being hunted by a grizzly, Skeen's view of life refocused to a colder outlook. A chill trickled through him. He thought the world even looked different, having been tinted with a gray film of fear.

Skeen was a tall, muscular man with long, black hair and dark, piercingly alert eyes. His deerskin clothing was topped by a loosely fitting, cat hide cloak. Fastened to a leather belt, he had a flint-bladed knife and a stone-headed club. A bow and quiver of arrows were strapped across his back. He carried two, flint-tipped spears.

While observing the rounded prints, including long indentations formed by claws, Skeen said to himself, during all of my previous life, I've thought I was a great hunter. This land is the place where I hunt. Now, with the discovery of bear tracks on top of my footprints in soft, swamp earth, I have become the hunted. The bear hunts for me the way I search for deer. I was trained to be an hunter just like the bear. Now I'm the hunted. I no longer see my surroundings as a place to search for game. I presently must see this land as an area that might conceal my enemy, the hump-backed grizzly. I know the bear is a persistent hunter. Once having a track, or scent, to follow, this enemy will try to pursue steadily until a kill is made. There are stories about people, from my village, being tracked and killed. Everything on the land fears this giant. Its spirit is a powerful presence. Most animals fear such an hunter. Wolves desert their pups when the grizzly approaches. I should not fear the giant because I belong to the clan of the bear and I wear its tooth on a thong around my neck. My father gave me this tooth and he got it from his father. Someone in my family, long ago, drilled an hole into this tooth. By passing a thong through the hole, my family's hunters have worn the tooth. Members of the bear clan have always been great hunters. The people of my village call me the Arrowmaker and I put my sign of the bear on everything I make. I sometimes chip arrow and spear points, or knives, in the form of a bear. I must not fear my hunting partner, the hump-backed grizzly. However, I have to be careful. Sometimes bears attack hunters because this great animal moves about without fear of anything. Some people who make arrows use the gray stone or soft, yellow stone. I prefer the shiny, easily flaked stone. I always put the design of the bear on everything I have made. I enjoy being called the Arrowmaker although I also make knives and spears. I use a point of the shiny, chipping stone to draw the form of a bear on everything. I scratched a form of a standing bear on the tooth I have tied by leather around my neck together with the shell amulet. The form of a bear actually makes a fine shape for an arrowhead, spear point or knife. I am thinking too much. I must be careful. I'm not just an hunter now. I have to be as wary as a deer. If a deer gets careless, the deer dies and is eaten by the hunter. I liked this land better when I was the hunter.

Skeen sat on a rock to rest while he considered his choices. Unlike the other deer, he said to himself, I am able to make more decisions. I can even decide to not be a deer. I could try to escape as others have tried before me. I could conceal my trail by walking in the water and return to our camping place at the cave. Since a bear can detect a person's scent from long distances, this hump-backed hunter does not have to find my tracks in order to find me. I also don't want to lead a bear to our camp where I first noticed the large tracks. There was a lot of joking in camp when I went picking berries with the women and girls rather than going hunting. I was just concerned about the safety of the women, considering the tracks I had seen near the berry patches. In camp, I'm known more as an arrow maker than an hunter. I think I'm skilled at being both an arrow maker and an hunter. If I had been known more as an hunter, I would've had a better chance to marry Shell. The last time I went on a long, hunting journey, Shell was given in marriage to the respected hunter, High Wolf. If Shell comes back to me, I'll know she didn't agree to this marriage and I will fight High Wolf. I'll be banished for fighting High Wolf; but I'll take Shell with me. If Shell stays with High Wolf, she will have made her decision. Some of the people said I went picking berries in order to visit Shell and people who said such things were right although I also went to protect the women. The villagers should not have talked about me so much and questioned my courage. High Wolf's friends questioned my hunting ability to help him marry Shell. Everything worked against me. Maybe Shell chose High Wolf. He is the best hunter. If she leaves him and comes to stay with me, I'll fight him and then be banished with Shell. If she stays with him, she will have made her own decision. Because Shell is beautiful in her own way, people talked about her. By questioning my hunting ability, the talkers helped High Wolf to marry Shell. I thought she would come back to me right away. However, so far, for one reason or another, she hasn't returned and her absence has tormented me. I can't stop thinking about her.

When I accompanied the berry pickers in order to protect them, I saw the great bear watching Shell. She saw it too. The bear, in the distance, looked like another person picking berries. When the bear moved toward Shell, she started running back to camp. She was exhausted when I reached her. Two of our dogs helped me stop the grizzly. With a deep, rumbling growl, the giant stood on its hind legs. A breeze rippled the creature's brown fur.

Remembering clearly the encounter with the bear, Skeen thought about the large animal as it pawed at the air in a gesture that seemed to say this hunter had no fear and all, or most, enemies were just nuisances or things to hunt. Sunlight shone on my spear shooting over the bear as the creature dropped downward and sprang toward me, Skeen recalled. It advanced with surprising speed. For some reason, there is a mistaken tendency to think a large animal can only move slowly. A paw swooped forward knocking a dog into some berry bushes. The bear chased the other dog. I found this dog later on the path. There had not been much of a fight and the dog had been partially eaten. Shell, particularly, along with some of the other women, called me and told me not to follow the grizzly. I had no choice. I had to do my best to protect the others.

The tracks were fresh and easy to follow. The paws were large. Claws put deep cuts in the earth. When I have a trail to check, I have to follow it. I learn much from tracks, marks or other signs. From such markings, I can see exactly what was happening as a print was marked in the earth, a root was torn from the ground or a chunk of bark was dislodged from a stump. I just naturally find myself wanting to follow any good trail.

I do much of my carving work when I'm away from the village. In the quite solitude of dawn, among the drops of water that catch the first rays of sunlight, I enjoy chipping the arrowheads, spear points or knives. I drilled an hole in a bear's tooth and gave it to Shell. On this tooth, I put my usual sign of a standing bear. She gave me the shell amulet.

Because I'm usually following trails or making arrows, away from the camp, people think I'm lazy and not much of an hunter. When I was away, arrangements were made for Shell to marry High Wolf. If she comes to stay with me, I will fight High Wolf then Shell and I will be banished. So far, she has not come to visit me. By not making a decision to visit me, she has made a decision to stay with High Wolf. I will fight him. I won't fight her. If that's what she wants, she'll have it. Also, if she doesn't act upon her decision, she has acted. We have to know when to drift with the directing currents and when to turn away from them.

I couldn't help following the bear. When such a trail is available, I have to follow it. I'm always checking trails or making arrows, spears and knives. On each object I make, I put my design of a standing bear. Some people think I'm lazy because I'm often—usually—away from camp. They don't realize I'm also an hunter like the other men who are more respected. Opinions of other people don't determine my character although these opinions helped arrange a marriage between Shell and High Wolf. I will not run from this fearsome bear. I also won't sit here and wait to be attacked. If I have an enemy following me, the only choice I have is to attack this enemy.

Skeen walked southeastward to higher terrain where he set up his hide shelter then kindled a fire. He had food with him although he was not yet hungry. He had eaten well at the cave camp and enjoyed another meal of meat and berries before the bear had attacked Shell along with the other people who had been picking berries.

I feel very much alone without my dog, reflected Skeen before he added more dry wood to a smokeless fire. The first dog killed by the bear had belonged to Shell. The other dog killed was not only my dog but he was my hunting companion. On my way back to our cave camp, I'll

return to the hill and visit the
wolf den that the bear had dug open.
If the wolves are still using the
site for a den, I'll get another pup
for myself and I'll also get one for
Shell to replace her dog. If I had
a dog—or wolf—with me now, such a
companion could help to tell me
where my enemy, the bear, is
located. Without a dog, I think I
see the bear in too many places. At
this time, the grizzly should be
farther east on my old trail. In
the first light of morning, I'll
walk farther southeast and wait for
my enemy. I hope he is tracking me
slowly so I can get some sleep
tonight.

Skeen watched flames flickering
across pieces of wood in his
campfire. Firelight danced toward
the surrounding swamp. He listened
to the night's sounds, hoping he
wouldn't hear a branch crack or a
twig snap. Wolves howled and a
mammoth trumpeted. Part of the pack
of wolves survived the grizzly's
attack, observed Skeen. Maybe other
wolves have already moved into this
area. Adult wolves always look
after any stray pups. I won't take
pups unless they seem to be in some
kind of trouble.

Watching firelight moving toward the swamp before fading among lurking shadows, Skeen recalled the campfires in the cave and the faces of the people as they told their stories. Many of the oldest people said they didn't like to hunt in the swamp. They said we should stay away from the swamp because, long ago when spruce trees were more plentiful and broad-leafed trees were scarcer, the big animals were much more abundant. After big animals had become scarce, we started hunting in the hidden places like the swamp. While we hunted in the swamp, we lost hunters. Hunters sometimes went out alone and didn't return. Places like the swamp are set aside for the protection of animals so they will not all be hunted and can renew themselves. There are spirits of the animals; but there is one, Great Spirit who protects the animals and is life itself.

Howls of wolves rang eerily through the murky swamp. A mammoth trumpeted again. Wolves are trying to tire a mammoth, noted Skeen while his eyes searched beyond the firelight, in the shadowy swamp, where each sound drove back the sleep he sought. He added a chunk of wood to the fire just before a shrill scream of an animal cut through the woods. This cry scraped along Skeen's nerves, leaving him fully alert, seeing the possible form of a bear amid each clump of shadows.

Flames swarmed along the new chunk of wood. Sparks swirled into the sky where dark forms of clouds removed the last traces of light. Wolves howled, filling the night with lingering cries that sent a shiver trickling down the back of Skeen's neck.

Watching firelight flickering toward the surrounding swamp, Skeen continued to be reminded of how similar light contorted the features of the woman's face, at the cave camp, when she said, "If you go to the swamp, watch out for the spring at the west end of the water. We used to go there to hunt mammoths in the shallow water. The clay earth can hold and trap a mammoth or an hunter. At the western end of the water, there is a deep spring. Much water bubbles out of this hole. My husband was killed there when a mammoth stumbled into the deep spring, thrashed around and then

12

rolled under the water for the last time. My husband got too close and was kicked by the struggling giant. We also hunted musk oxen in a grassy area west of the spring. Watch out for the swamp because, particularly in that place, I could sense the presence of the Mysterious One who protects all life including animals. We only hunted in the swamp when we were hungry. If we were hungry, we had success. If we were not hungry, we had trouble."

Skeen could not sleep. Wolves howled in the swamp. They were coming closer. The wolves are tiring a mammoth, Skeen told himself. They kill the great beast with fatigue. The one who tires first does not eat. I must not waste my energy. Since I can't sleep, I'll look for the bear.

Checking surrounding shadows for one that looked like a bear and moved, Skeen recalled the face of the elder as she said, "One time, an hunter was stalked by a bear near a large boulder close to our camp. The bear chased the man who ran around the rock. In this chase, the bear tired first then the man speared the bear."

Clouds drifted eastward, revealing a sickle moon in a starlit sky. With the help of this light, I could continue traveling, Skeen said to himself. I can't sleep anyway. Sleep does not come to me because my mind is too busy thinking about stories and also my enemy, the great bear. I'll check my old tracks and see what my enemy is doing.

He walked southeast toward higher ground overlooking the route he had taken to reach the swamp. He heard a loud splashing sound coming from the north before he sat down on the trunk of a fallen birch. From out of a break in the bark, a snake appeared. The serpent slithered quickly out of pale moonlight and vanished among shadows.

After watching the snake move away, Skeen left the trunk and sat down on a smooth rock. He rested while watching his back trail. Nothing ominous appeared to be disturbing the solitude. Maybe the bear has already passed this area and is now behind me, Skeen warned himself. That's a chilling possibility. Maybe I think too much and worry far too often. I could walk over and check my tracks to see if an enemy has been following me.

However I don't want my fresh tracks to reveal my present position. I'm safe if I stay here and watch for the bear unless this hunter is behind me.

My life so far has been somewhat successful, mused Skeen while he rested and watched the forest. I am a respected arrow maker. I'm called Arrowmaker. I also make spears and knives. On all things I make, I put my design of the standing bear. I have failed regarding Shell. Due to my inaction, or her preference, she is now with High Wolf. He knows I always considered Shell to be my wife. Therefore High Wolf and I are natural enemies. He might be thinking that I would try to get Shell back. Of course, I'll try to get her away from him although she makes her own decisions. Maybe she agreed to this arrangement with High Wolf, or possibly this situation was forced upon her. People often don't have a choice. I know I have two enemies. High Wolf is my enemy and so is this great, hump-backed bear.

Skeen didn't move. He waited with the patience of a skilled hunter. There were the usual sounds and movements of the night. Noting the faint breeze snaking through swamp from the east, he thought, if the bear is approaching me along my old trail, that breeze will take my scent away from this enemy. If the bear is behind or beside me, the breeze will reveal my scent. If the bear is behind me, this animal will have another advantage.

The thought of a breeze disclosing his position to a bear approaching from behind in the night, started to unsettle Skeen until the lone man wondered if he was seeing a bear disturbing a moving leaf, standing next to a stump or lurking among shadows. I am alone in the Spirit Swamp, Skeen said to himself. The giant, hump-backed hunter is following me at night. Maybe my other enemy, High Wolf, is also here. I'm worrying too much.

As time dragged on toward the first, pale colors of dawn, all of Skeen's worries settled in his stomach when, along his old trail, he saw a man standing. This man was very large and, because of the person's cat skin cape, Skeen recognized High Wolf. Upon identifying High Wolf, Skeen realized he had already made the

largest mistake he could make
because he was staring at this
enemy. High Wolf had stopped and
was watching Skeen. Both enemies
had detected each other. High Wolf
started walking directly toward
Skeen.

High Wolf walked with an angry,
determined step. He knocked
branches out of his way, using a
club in one hand and a knife in his
other hand. Between himself and his
new wife, Shell, there was always
the presence of Skeen. Skeen could
be killed now, away from the cave
camp.

Skeen fitted an arrow to the
sinew string of his bow. He pulled
back the string, aimed the arrow
then shot it. It whooshed slightly
away from its target and went
completely through the side of High
Wolf's cape. He groaned deeply and
dropped his knife. He moved his
hand and found he could continue to
use his hand and arm. The arrow had
cut his arm while passing through
the cape.

High Wolf sidestepped to avoid
the second arrow. It stuck into the
trunk of a tree behind him. He felt
the feathers of the third shaft as
it passed his neck and went through

his cape.   Arrows will not stop me now, High Wolf thought as the fourth shaft cut some skin on his side. He used his club to deflect the fifth arrow shot at him.   Then he ran forward and grabbed Skeen in a bear hug that attempted to force the life out of this enemy.

Skeen shot his knee up into the man's crotch, leaving the fat giant grimacing with pain. Without taking time to turn the spear around to be able to apply the stone-tipped end, Skeen jabbed the wooden end of his shaft upward along the man's chest and head. Then Skeen used the spear like a club and slammed it against High Wolf's head. The large man's face flushed with anger. He raised his club, using both hands. The man's eyes stared and became glazed. His face paled. Skeen just watched this enemy as, incredulously, he turned and ran back toward the trail.   Following the large man's hasty retreat, Skeen relaxed and was puzzled as to what had suddenly put such fear in his enemy's heart.

Skeen heard something scrape across the fallen, birch trunk. Whirling around to face another enemy, Skeen saw the massive outline of the great bear. The creature was standing in front of the trunk. The jaws opened before the head moved from side to side. A bellowing roar came from the creature's throat.

Mustering all his strength, Skeen shot his spear at the dark form. As the shaft was released from Skeen's hand, the bear moved forward, growling, and the shaft whispered over the creature's head. Flashing ponderously large paws and issuing guttural growls, the bear charged. Skeen was at first paralyzed by the sight of this creature approaching as if it had come out of a dream. Skeen hoped the charge was a bluff like others he had seen from other bears. Most of his thoughts became riveted to the fact that this charge was not a bluff. The animal kept advancing. Skeen reached for a second spear then he glimpsed a blurred motion of a paw coming from the side before he saw a flash of light and he lost consciousness.

Skeen woke up in darkness. Brush was on top of him. Sunlight sparkled through openings in the pile of vegetation. Pain throbbed in his head. The bear has buried me under brush, saving me for a later meal, Skeen said to himself. A swipe of the paw hit me on the side of my head.

Pushing the foliage away slowly, Skeen was relieved to discover that no bones had been broken. He could use his arms and was also able to move his legs.

He stood up amid the brush. Although his head ached, he felt exulted about his additional chance to live. The bear must not have been hungry and buried me to save this meal for another time, thought Skeen. The great, hump-backed hunter will be angry when it discovers its food has walked away. I'm going to walk away now.

First Skeen retrieved his weapons then he looked at the surrounding forest where sunlight dropped in wedges through an high canopy of foliage. I'm lucky to have this second chance to live, he said to himself. I won't get such a chance again. Rather than just being alive, I must start enjoying life and put it to some sort of good use. I don't like to kill animals, birds or fish. I only hunt to get enough food. Like the bear, I don't kill unless I'm getting food. The bear is an hunter like me. I am a member of the bear clan. This

animal is much like me, yet
sometimes it can become a great
adversary. We are both hunters and
members of this swamp. Without the
bear, my life in the swamp would be
less worrisome although emptier.
The hump-backed hunter has a
powerful spirit. I am aware of this
spirit's presence. It guides me and
also can harm me if I get careless.
This swamp is greater because of the
presence of the bear.

Skeen walked most of the day
along a winding route. He doubled
back often and waded through ponds
in an attempt to not leave behind a
trail of scent that could easily be
followed. I'm starting to think too
much like the hunted and not enough
like an hunter, he told himself as
he prepared a camp among trees close
to the spring. He unwrapped
smoldering embers to start a fire.
From his pack, he also removed a
chunk of musk oxen meat. In a short
time, he was enjoying the fragrance
of roasting meat while the meat
cooked on the end of a stick held
over the flames. A forked, upright
stake supported the stick that
skewered the meat. With meat
roasting over the fire, this day and
my new life both look better to me,

reflected Skeen after he sat down beside his fire and turned the meat so it would cook evenly.

He greeted the evening with fresh enthusiasm. Although the day was vanishing among gathering shadows, his life was new again. He saw everything from the view of his second chance to live. Now that I'm starting over again, I am able to change things, he mused. During my first life, I was not aggressive enough with my enemies because I let them take away Shell. To get her back, I would have to fight and kill High Wolf. That's maybe what I must do.

Using his hands and the flint knife, Skeen removed large chunks of steaming, fragrant meat. He added a film of white ashes for flavor. He chewed the meat slowly and enjoyed a sense of contentment. He relaxed then slept until the next morning. After rekindling his fire, he reheated the musk ox meat.

He welcomed the rays of sunlight dropping through openings in foliage. Caught in this light, innumerable droplets of moisture glimmered throughout the swamp. An hawk screamed from a pink sky above the treetops.

Like the bear, the hawk only kills when it needs something to eat, observed Skeen. Real hunters don't waste life by killing creatures if food is not needed.

Skeen checked his weapons. Using damp sinew, he tied a freshly chipped, stone point to the end of a spear. This stone point, like all of his other weapons, contained the design of a standing bear. Having checked his equipment, he walked to the other distant swamp. He walked through a region of seemingly endless rushes until he reached the widening of the stream. Using a stone club and a prying pole, he broke off chunks of the shiny, gray stone. He put much of this stone in his pack. Next he uncovered the pottery bowl that Shell had made. He used it to cook stew consisting of clams and roots.

While relaxing beside his fire, he employed a finely formed piece of stone to etch outlines of standing bears on some of his recently chipped arrow points. He worked in light from the fire then slept in his hide shelter.

The next day, Skeen returned to his other camping place near the spring. He rebuilt his fire and continued working on his new pieces of stone. He enjoyed his camp and rested before sleeping beside his fire.

In the morning, he greeted the new day and resolved again to make the most of his second chance at life. He rebuilt his fire and started roasting a chunk of musk ox meat.

After collecting extra firewood and piling this wood beside his sleeping place, he sat down and continued turning the stick holding the meat over the flames so the food would cook evenly. I must go to the hill and see if I can get any wolf pups, he said to himself. If I get only one pup, I'll give it to Shell to replace her dog killed by the bear. If there are two pups, I'll keep one for myself. I like to have a dog with me. They are good company and great hunters. High Wolf will go back and tell Shell the great bear killed me. I must return to our cave camp so the people will know I am alive and, some day, I'm going to reclaim Shell as my wife. Of course, judging by everything she has done, she has decided to stay with High Wolf.

Reaching for a strand of hide circling his neck and holding the tooth and shell pendants, he clasped the shell and thought, this pendant brought me good luck as Shell said it would. She said the pendant had been a carrier of luck for previous hunters in her family. Apparently one of her ancestors had traded two prized fishhooks to get this unusual shell. It looks like a wolf's head and Shell is a member of the wolf clan.

Out from the cover of trees to the northwest, beyond the spring, lumbered an aged mammoth. The creature seemed to be battle weary and was followed by four wolves. They circled the beleaguered giant and snapped at its feet. This struggle had apparently been raging for a long time because the mammoth's movements were strained, slow and awkward. Although stumbling occasionally, the creature stomped its large feet in soft, clay earth and swung long, curved tusks at the attackers. Blood sprayed from gashes on the giant's legs. From the trail of blood, the wolves smelled victory and remained persistent although wary. This battle moved into the water.

The giant is losing much blood, thought Skeen as he watched a large leg try unsuccessfully to stomp a wolf. The mammoth's life is flowing away along with the blood, noted Skeen. The wolves know the blood will eventually lead to a great amount of food.

The mammoth fell in shallow water. When a wolf moved forward to gnaw on the creature's belly, a massive, front foot shot forward and knocked the attacker lifelessly into a thicket of bulrushes. The giant rolled onto its stomach, eliminating a second gnawing wolf while thrusting tusks killed a third attacker. Three other wolves came from the western, grassy region and accompanied the survivor. These four wolves continued to watch the mammoth.

Skeen added green wood and leaves to his fire, making extra smoke to drive away the mosquitoes. An ache in his head persisted along with an heavy feeling of fatigue. Such feelings had accompanied him after his battle with the bear. Weariness seeped through his consciousness while the excitement of recent events fought to keep him awake. He sat next to his fire and again turned the stick skewered through the meat.

While the meat cooked slowly, Skeen watched the swamp. Large, open areas of water mirrored surrounding greenery. A shadow of a circling vulture glided across the water. At the western edge of the water, grasses were mixed with flowers. The eastern shoreline contained areas of dense foliage. Northward, the land ascended to the top of an hill etched against an azure sky where clouds drifted.

Other hunters said a bear had dug out a wolf den on the side of the hill beside the swamp, recalled Skeen. I must visit this den and see if I can locate a pup for Shell and one for myself. However, I have to travel slowly because of my headaches and I seem to get tired much too easily. After resting for a while, I'll try to get two pups and return to our cave camp. High Wolf will have told our camp that the great bear killed me in the swamp. If Shell thinks I'm dead, she will stay with High Wolf. He possibly really thinks I was killed because the bear is a great hunter and tracker. Usually nothing escapes from this giant and it is likely hunting me now. I must be careful; yet I am weary. I have to rest before I attempt to get two pups and return to our camp at the cave. Adult wolves always look after any pups. If adult wolves are taking care of the pups, I will not try to take them.

Wolves howled and the mammoth thrashed in the shallow water. The mammoth will be getting very weak because of losing so much blood, noted Skeen after he removed the meat from the skewer. The steaming meat was juicy and flavorful. He chewed this food slowly.

Having enjoyed much of the delicious meat, Skeen wanted to drink some water. He left his camp and walked toward bulrushes and grasses extending westward. Plants rippled and shimmered as a gentle breeze stirred through the swamp. A sweet fragrance of grasses drifted with the breeze when Skeen approached the water. The clay earth was slippery in some areas. Black muck covered other sections.

The old ones, recalled Skeen, said they hunted mammoths in shallow water at the edge of the swamp. They said hunters had to be wary of the western shoreline because the spring was deep and dangerous. "Don't go hunting in the swamp unless you really need food," the storyteller had said. "Don't hunt in the swamp unless you really need food because birds and animals require such places to hide and find protection in order to live. At the western end of the water, the spring is in a deep hole. Cold water bubbles out of a large opening in clay and sand. Animals as well as people can get stuck in this clay."

Skeen noticed that the water along the shoreline was an amber color. The deep area, where water bubbled out of the ground, was a darker brown and almost black. Farther out in the swamp, the water reflected a bluish color from the sky. There was also a greenish hue mirrored from surrounding foliage along with a golden shimmer added by sunlight. All the colors of the swamp seemed to blend together in a flash of resplendent beauty. Surely this is a place where animals can come to find protection from hunters, observed Skeen.

He waded through shallow water until he was close to the spring with its bubbling water stirring the calm surface. To drink some of this cold water, he kneeled down on both knees and lowered his face to the clear surface. Something moving beside him caught his attention and he noticed a turtle swimming under the water. The turtle's head broke through the surface, got some air then withdrew to lower depths, leaving behind a few remnant bubbles. Farther away, a snake's head sliced through the pond's surface forming a trail of ripples.

Wolf howls diverted Skeen's attention northward to the dark form of the mammoth. The creature had stopped moving and resembled one of the islands amid the water, grasses, bulrushes, bushes and trees of the swamp. Wolves had been gorging themselves on the immense supply of food and howled somewhat indifferently at Skeen.

The howling wolves near the mammoth were answered by an howl from the west. Knowing wolves well, Skeen turned to see what had caught the interest of the more distant wolf. Grasses rippled in a breeze that had changed direction and fitfully stirred toward the west were grasses where topped by a jagged outline of spruce trees. An herd of musk oxen had entered the flat area to graze on grass. A young bull had apparently detected a worrisome scent and was coming directly toward Skeen. The young bull could see wolves, yet seemed to not be concerned about them. The bull had picked up Skeen's scent and was following it without turning away. With increasing speed, the musk ox kept advancing, coming directly at Skeen.

Trapped by the spring, Skeen ran southward toward the trees near his camp. When he raced for a spruce tree, the bull followed. Skeen's throat dried, his heart pounded and his mind filled with thrashing sounds of the charging, bull musk ox. Skeen risked taking a quick glance behind and saw water spraying away from an onrushing form looming out of the greenish colored swamp topped by blue sky.

Skeen reached a spruce just before the bull hit the opposite side amid a cracking and thrashing of branches. When the large head slashed from one side to another inside the outer canopy of branches, Skeen scrambled upward along the trunk. He broke off small branches to clear a path for climbing. The aggressive animal slammed into the trunk, jolting Skeen roughly and almost dislodging him. Looking down, he saw the musk ox as it left the tree then stopped to watch for any other threat. Aggression seemed to have been sufficiently released. He walked slowly toward other musk oxen in the grassy region west of the swamp.

Skeen's head throbbed with pain. He tried to relax; however he was weary and trembled as a chill coursed through him. The trunk and its branches supported him securely. He kept trying to relax and he welcomed sleep.

He was awakened the next morning by a breeze stirring through foliage. A pink sky brightened in the east. Rays of sunlight shot across the horizon, sending wedges of light through mist rising from the swamp. The pink sky turned ominously red before brightening again.

From his resting-place in the tree, Skeen looked for, yet could not see, the aggressive, bull musk ox. Skeen's patience was stronger than the thirst that dried his throat. Hunger also gripped his stomach. He waited and enjoyed the warming sunlight while a fitful breeze stirred foliage.

This swamp is full of life, he reflected. Since hunters do not come here unless they are very hungry, the animals have a place to live as well as renew themselves and hunters have a region where they can get food in times of great shortage. I came here only because the bear was threatening the berry pickers. I must return to our cave village. I think the Mysterious One makes places like this swamp to protect the life of the land. Time doesn't bring much change to these spirit places. A person must come to such areas with respect. I feel very close to the spirit world here. Maybe I am soon to enter this spirit life that does not end. Before I enter the spirit world, there are things I want to do on this land. I must return to my village so the people will know I am still alive and I want to reclaim Shell as my wife. I wonder if she left with High Wolf because she wanted to leave with him or because she was tricked when I was away hunting. I must reclaim my wife. I know at least now I have an enormous thirst.

I must go to the spring and get a drink.

Only the breeze moved along grasses on the western side of the water. There was a sweet fragrance coming from this grass. If the musk oxen were present, they were not in sight. The tree was starting to feel particularly uncomfortable and confining. His mouth had dried a long time ago. He had to get water from the spring.

The mammoth died near the spring, thought Skeen. Three wolves died also. Animals have died here along with people. This watery place is a refuge and offers protection to animals. Hunters come here to get food when food can't be found in the surrounding region. The swamp is a spiritual place where animals and people rejoin the spirit to walk along the everlasting trail and come back again. In such a location as this the spirit is more noticeable. I can almost see the Mysterious One walking through here in the form of the birds, animals and people. They all die to rejoin the spirit before they come back again and they are just changing forms of the one spirit. All of us and every thing are part of the

Mysterious One. I'm just coming to know the spirit of the swamp. I am seeing the spirit more all the time. Maybe I'm on my way to the spirit and I won't, for a long time, get back to the cave camp to reclaim my wife. Life does not stop. It only goes to the spiritual form then can come back here. Life continues. There can't, therefore, be mistakes because there are only delays. I sense I'm close to the spirit and might be delayed on my journey to reclaim my wife.

Stepping from one branch to another while his hands held other branches, Skeen carefully moved down the tree's trunk. He looked for the musk ox. Since the bull was not in sight, Skeen stepped onto the ground and started walking toward the spring. Sunlight added yellow tints to the green hues of grasses rippled by a morning breeze. Stepping on firm, clay earth felt comforting to Skeen compared to climbing along the narrow, spruce branches. He walked through sweetly scented grasses and reached the water at the edge of the spring.

Being careful to not get stuck in slippery clay, he drank cold water. It sent a shiver through him and helped to revive his strength. Much of his weariness dissolved. Afterward, he bathed in the refreshing water. He used gritty clay for cleansing.

After washing slowly and replacing his leather clothing, he felt renewed when he looked around at the bright, new day. He heard splashing and pounding sounds of something coming directly toward him. Looking back, he saw water spraying away from the charging form of the bull, musk ox.

Having no time to run to the right or left, Skeen dove into the stirring depths of the spring. He opened his eyes and, through murky greenish-amber water, he saw rugged, clay forms.

He returned to the surface to get air just as the bull was trying to both stop and turn on the slippery clay. The animal flipped over in a splashing, leg-flailing crash. Almost as part of the same movement, the bull was back on its feet and watching Skeen. The exertions of the charge and tumble seemed to have been sufficient to burn off most of the creature's aggressiveness. Moving slowly, the bull walked toward dark forms of other musk oxen grazing on the grassy region to the west.

Skeen swam to shore. He picked up his weapons then returned to his camp where he rebuilt the fire. With his clothes drying slowly and a fragrance of sizzling meat drifting through camp, Skeen sat down on elevated ground at the western side of his fire. He felt all his tenseness dissolve into the recesses of welcome sleep. He woke up in darkness. He savored the last of the roasted meat before he checked his weapons. He added wood to the fire's embers and slept until the next morning. He was awakened by something moving beside him. He sensed this movement more than he heard it. The cause of his concern came into view in the form of a snake emerging from the earth next to the sleeping mat of boughs. Skeen found himself staring at an uplifted, snake's head. Skeen screamed as he stabbed his spear through the creature. It writhed around the piercing shaft. The second spear thrust impaled the serpent twice before the coils stopped squirming.

Holding the shafts of his two spears, he carried the impaled snake

away from camp and dropped the dark
form into tall grass. He used grass
to remove blood from his spears.
Afterward, he returned to his camp.
Mist hung in warm air. A slight
breeze stirred mist along with
leaves and grasses.

Skeen reached for the thong
around his neck and suddenly
realized his necklace along with its
wolf-head shell and the tooth with
an etching of a standing bear were
missing. I must have lost my shell
and tooth when I swam away from the
musk ox, Skeen thought. Shell gave
me the wolf-head shell for good luck
in hunting. She said the pendant
would also protect me like it had
helped other hunters in her family.
I'll ask her for another shell
protector although I don't think
protection really comes from such
objects. They give us guidance only
because they remind us of the
Mysterious One and direct our
thoughts to the spirit world. My
spirit reminders are now in the
spring and it is spiritual place.
Maybe these objects, being in such a
location, will be like continuing
prayers and will bring me good
fortune. This swamp is a form of
the spirit and has been placed here

for a refuge to be used by birds, animals and people. I strongly feel the presence of the spirit here. Maybe that's a sign my time has come to return to the spirit realm. I feel drawn away although I don't want to leave until my life is in order. I lost my shell and tooth reminders of luck. The real luck comes in realizing there is no such thing as luck because everything is planned. I wonder if, in the plan of the Mysterious One, I will have to wait to put my life in order at a different time. I will return to the spirit and then I'll know if I can come back at another time to complete my work and my life. All things are happening at once, at the same time, because, if time has no end, there are no time divisions. All apparent divisions are taking place as part of the same time. If I get back to my cave village, I'll ask the old ones about such things. If I don't get back, I will have returned to the spirit in this swamp and I'll have answers to my questions.

Daylight was brightening the swamp. Shafts of light shot through openings in foliage and emblazoned twisting tendrils of drifting mist.

Sunlight illuminated drops of dew, changing them to lights shimmering throughout the watery forest. I know the Mysterious One has a special presence in places like this swamp, Skeen reflected after he checked his equipment. I must ask the old ones. I know, in this place, I am in a special presence of the Mysterious One. The swamp is stirring itself, getting ready for another day. If I don't leave now, my spirit will rejoin the spirit of the swamp and I have work to do with my life here before I enter the spirit world.

Carrying his spears, while having a bow and quiver of arrows looped across his back, Skeen left his camp. He walked northwest toward the spring. Because he couldn't see the musk oxen, he decided to get a drink of water to prepare for a long walk. I'll travel to the hills and see if I can get two pups before I journey farther westward to the caves among high rocks beside the great lake. The hump-backed bear dug out the wolf den. Maybe I will be able to get some pups. I hope the bear is not continuing to hunt for me.

Skeen walked to the spring. Its water reflected a pale sky and surrounding foliage. He watched this beauty until it became all he knew. It entered him or drew him to itself and he was filled with its spirit.

He was watching the water when he heard the splashing sounds. He turned around to see what was causing this disturbance and he saw the great, hump-backed bear approaching rapidly. The bear was bounding forward as if pleased to have relocated a missing meal.

Skeen tried to fight back a flash of nervous tension while he removed the bow from his shoulder. He took an arrow from the quiver and fitted this shaft to the string made of twisted sinew. He shot the arrow quickly. When it stuck in the bear's neck, the animal growled and slapped at the shaft, breaking it. Splinters of wood dropped into foaming water kicked upward by large, swiftly moving paws. A second arrow lodged in the bear's shoulder. The animal growled again and slapped the shaft away as if it was a biting fly. The bear's anger flared after a third arrow stuck just below the neck. Issuing a guttural growl, the giant increased its momentum and raged forward, running furiously with all possible speed.

The first spear hit the bear's chest. This shaft slowed the charge because the animal had more trouble dislodging the stronger wood. The bear stopped and clawed at this painful thing. The paw hit the protruding section of the broken spear and drove it completely into the chest. This blow enraged the animal. It roared with pain and blood sprayed from the injury.

The hump-backed hunter stumbled. It stopped, gathered strength and charged. When the animal moved forward, it approached a raised spear. The weapon was thrust upward guided by all of Skeen's skill and strength. The spear's point sank into the large body but couldn't stop the jaws and impact of the massive animal. It hit Skeen, covered him and both hunters went into the spring.

The spring's water thrashed at first before boiling then stirring until remnant ripples gradually dissipated, leaving the surface again with a reflection of the

foliage,   forms   and   life   of   the
swamp.

Daniel Hance Page

TWO

NIGHT STAR

1600

After being banished from his Dakota village because he had killed a chief, Winter Hawk traveled far to the east, hoping he would meet the Dakota's old enemies, the Ojibways. Winter Hawk planned to either fight these enemies or join them. I have no choice, he told himself. I've been banished from my village. The only other people I know are our enemies, the Ojibways. I can fight them as I have before. Maybe I will join them and fight the Dakota who are now also my enemies.

Winter Hawk was a lean man of medium height. He had received a facial injury during a battle. The resulting scar gave his face a perpetual scowl and also left him with only one eye. His two accomplices during the killing of the chief, where High Back and Red Hand. High Back was a skulking man who was always grimacing as if his mind was grappling with a thought that would bring harm to someone. Red Hand was a short, scruffy man who would help with any fight as long as he thought he was on the winning side.

The three men walked silently and in single file. Winter Hawk pushed on ahead while his snowshoes whispered across fine snow. High Back came second followed by Red Hand. They traveled steadily eastward across a winter landscape under a cold, pale sky. A few old tracks made by Ojibways had been noted in the snow. These snowshoe prints indicated the presence of an Ojibway family consisting of a man and a woman.

Eastward of the three advancing Dakotas, there was the camp of the Ojibway hunter, Black Fox, and his wife, Night Star. Black Fox usually wore his fox cape along with a bear skin cloak over his deerskin clothing. Although he was a young man, the snows and difficulties of some harsh winters left lines on his face. During this particular winter, game had been scarce and he had traveled southward toward the swamp. The area provided food during times of shortages. Good water always flowed from the spring.

Black Fox had been to the spring on other occasions when

hunting had been difficult farther north. Mostly, however, he liked to travel south to the spring in times of need because of his grandmother's legends. They told of the special place where an hunter could always find game if his family was short of food.

Black Fox and his wife had hunted successfully in the swamp. With a good supply of meat and furs, Black Fox and Night Star were ready to return to the north to their traditional, winter hunting area beside the Shebeshekong River. Here, along rock ledges beside the river, there remained a small quantity of wild rice cached in stone storage areas topped by logs and slabs of rock. The extra food obtained from the swamp, along with the stored rice, would get the family through the winter.

Before traveling north to the traditional, winter camp, Black Fox persuaded his wife to accompany him on another journey. He wanted to first go to the west to visit caves described by his grandmother. Night Star had agreed with this plan and, before returning to the Shebeshekong River, they walked toward the caves.

A small fire flickered in the wigwam. Black Fox waited for his wife, Night Star, to return from checking her snares. He smoked his pipe and recalled the stories told by his grandmother. "If you are short of food," she said, "go south to the swamp. It is southeast of Reed Lake. The Willow River flows into Reed Lake. On the south bank of Willow River, you will find the place where Spring Creek enters the river. If you follow the creek upstream, you will come to a spring-fed pond in Spirit Swamp. This pond is large. It is fed by spring water that bubbles out of an underwater opening in the finest, pottery-making clay. The spring is at the western end of the pond, almost at its edge. Because of the movement of water flowing out of the spring, the ice during winter never freezes well above this current.

The swamp is a great hunting area. I think the Great Spirit sets aside such regions for wildlife to find refuge and replenish themselves. Without such refuges, there would likely be no wildlife. For each thing on earth, there is a place and a purpose. All things are different aspects of the Great

Spirit. We must resect life and its environment because both are connected. We have to live respectfully. Do not hunt in the swamp unless you really need food.

West of Spirit Swamp, there are caves. Visit them if you have time. People lived there a long time ago. On walls of these caves, there are drawings. One drawing was of the hump-backed grizzly. A few of these bears continue to live in our region today. Most bears are black. Some grizzlies are also here.

The caves are a good place to stay if you need a camp. They are located on high ground. From them, you can see much of the surrounding region. In these caves, there are deep places where there is ice even during the summer. Such cold rooms make good areas for storing meat.

The old people who hunted here and lived in those caves are maybe, to some extent, our ancestors. However, our people say we came from the east a long time ago. We came from a region where there was salt water. Maybe we traveled west particularly because the Iroquois were coming from the south and moving northward."

Black Fox often let his thoughts drift back to the legends told by his grandmother. He added wood to his fire, feeding a small flame flickering across a bed of embers. He always enjoyed the warmth and light provided by a fire. He kept the fire burning steadily without much smoke. My wife must be out for a long walk and not just checking snares, he said to himself. If she is away much longer, I'll have to look for her. She is adventurous, like me. We have been through an hard winter. There was no game around our northern camp. We were running short of wild rice. The stone, storage bins beside the river have been used for a long time by our people. Maybe the first people who lived here and used the caves also built these bins. I enjoy living in the valley beside the stone storehouses. The river, winding through the valley, provides us with water and fish. Sometimes deer, moose and other animals are also plentiful. We ran short of food this winter. We have obtained a good supply of meat in the swamp. After visiting the caves, we will go back north to our winter camp in the valley.

Black Fox put tobacco in his clay pipe. Using a burning stick from the fire, he lit the tobacco and watched a tendril of smoke wind toward the openings at the top of the wigwam. Night Star has been out a long time, he reflected. That's not unusual for her. She pulls a well-equipped toboggan and she can shoot a bow and arrow well. I shouldn't worry about her.

Inside the wigwam, a fragrance of tobacco smoke mingled with a scent of wood smoke and a pungent resign from the hemlock, bough mattress. When Night Star returns, we must start traveling the next day, Black Fox told himself. I want to visit the caves my grandmother described then we will return to our valley. We have lots of meat now and furs. Grandmother said we should not hunt in the swamp unless we are very short of food. We have respected her advice. Because deer gather in the swamp during the winter, hunting was easy. Rabbits were also plentiful. We obtained fox and black bear furs. We got one grizzly and a caribou. I didn't realize caribou came this far south.

West of Black Fox's wigwam, a prevailing northerly wind had formed a sharply edged snowdrift. Above this snowdrift, there appeared a grotesquely smiling apparition of a skinned wolf's face. The wolf hide continued moving upward, revealing the garishly painted and twisted face of Winter Hawk. He quickly noted the camp and its surroundings then he turned and walked westward. Behind him, a light breeze moved snowflakes along the drift as if to erase any lingering presence of the unwelcome visitor.

Winter Hawk returned to a camp hidden by cedars. In this camp, High Back and Red Hand were sitting beside the warming flames of a smokeless fire. Winter Hawk also sat beside the fire. Without speaking, Red Hand gave Winter Hawk a chunk of smoked moose meat. The three men chewed meat silently. Firelight jumped across painted faces along with fur cloaks and deerskin clothing.

An owl, gliding above the treetops, veered sharply away from cedars where three men sat beside a fire. After chewing some meat, Winter Hawk said to the other men, "The tracks lead to one wigwam ahead of us. In this lodge, there is one man and a woman. We will have an easy victory and get lots of furs and meat. No one has come out of the lodge for a long time. They must be sleeping. Since they are sleeping, Red Hand will enter the wigwam and kill them."

Deepening background hues of evening added brightness to flames flickering in front of the painted faces. Occasional sparks from dry, cedar wood swirled upward within the darkening greenery of the cedar enclosure.

"What if they are not sleeping?" asked Red Hand.

"You will then run out," answered Winter Hawk. "When they chase you, High Back and I will kill them. If they don't chase you, we will burn their lodge to force them to come out. I would prefer to not have to burn their equipment that we can have for ourselves."

"Should we wait for first light in the morning to use your plan?" asked High Back.

"They are sleeping now," replied Winter Hawk. He looked around at the other two painted faces. There were no further questions. Sparks drifted upward while the three men checked flint knives, flint-tipped arrows and spears along with stone-headed tomahawks.

Winter Hawk left the camp. High Back, as usual, walked second, followed by Red Hand. The first two men concealed themselves behind the western snowdrift. Red Hand stepped toward the quiet wigwam. Although his throat was dry and his heart pounded, he pushed himself onward. He had entered such quiet lodges previously. He tried to turn his fear into alertness for battle. He kept advancing because approaching the lodge was better than fighting Winter Hawk. Winter Hawk and High Back should go first at least once, he thought.

The hooting of an owl startled Red Hand. Thinking this call might have awakened the people in the lodge, he rushed forward, pulled aside the hide that covered the entrance and entered a murky structure. Light from a small flame moved shadows ominously. Shadows partially hid the lodge's occupant before he forced the spear upward into Red Hand's midsection. Issuing a guttural groan, Red Hand grasped the spear. He staggered out of the lodge and fell backwards. His form remained still on the snow while a feathered shaft slanted upward from his body.

Silence gripped the winter camp before the form of a large man sprang out through the wigwam's entranceway. Arrows shot by Winter Hawk and High Back whizzed through cold, night air and stuck in this large man. He shot one arrow toward his enemies then another shaft hit him and he fell onto the snow.

Holding tomahawks, Winter Hawk and High Back scrambled passed the fallen form and entered the lodge. When they left the structure, after a short interval, they carried bundles of furs, food and equipment.

An owl hooted occasionally from a white pine while the two men worked in the camp. Having tied bundles to a toboggan, they entered the lodge. They sat comfortably beside a small, warming fire and ate roasted, caribou meat. Filled with food and weary from their efforts, they relaxed then slept in the lodge.

The two sleeping men didn't hear the owl hooting when the form of Night Star approached the wigwam. Stricken with grief upon seeing her husband lying on the snow, she pulled him to a place hidden by cedars.

Before returning to the wigwam, she checked her toboggan and equipment. She took the loaded toboggan to a concealed site west of the wigwam. If she had to leave in an hurry, she could rush back to get her loaded toboggan and it would be ready for traveling.

Night Star was a slim woman of medium height. She wore a bear cloak over her other deerskin clothing. Her black, alert eyes watched for any movement in the pale night. Nothing stirred. The resonant hooting of an owl startled her.

Snowshoe tracks of three men approached my wigwam, she said to herself while she walked toward the lodge. There are no tracks leaving my home. Two men are inside. A wisp of smoke comes from the openings at the top of my wigwam. Not much fire is burning. The men must be sleeping. They will not know how many people are with me. They won't try to pursue me immediately although they will follow me.

The owl hooted. Night Star watched as the broad-winged bird

left the white pine and flew into the murky sky. The owl's faint shadow flickered across the snow before Night Star's spear pushed aside the hide covering the entranceway.

Inside the compact shelter, two men seemed to be sleeping beside a remnant flame on embers in a fire pit. One man's hand pulled a tomahawk from his belt and he stood up. When Night Star's spear impaled this man, his mouth opened, although no sound came from him. His eyes bulged on his astonished face. Grasping the shaft in his hands, he fell onto the embers.

The second man, who had a twisted face, kicked Night Star's legs out from under her sending her tumbling onto her back. This man, holding a knife, loomed over her. She kicked him in the crotch then picked up an adjacent bundle of furs and pounded them into the man's face. When he fell over backwards, she sprang out of the lodge. Running at a steady pace, she returned to her loaded toboggan. She pulled it behind her and walked rapidly westward. Before he comes after me, he will wait to see how many enemies he has encountered, she reasoned. I could've tried to kill him when he fell; however, instead, I saw a chance to escape and ran. I think I did the right thing. I'm alive and I can take care o' myself. I'll go to the caves to carry out my husband's dream. If this enemy continues to pursue me, I will seek refuge in the swamp before I turn northward and go home to my winter camp in the valley.

Night Star continued walking until dawn's gray light seeped slowly across the land. She felt as cold, empty and bleak as the view before her. She was not tired because she was accustomed to walking long distances. Her grief obscured the thought of resting and allowed her to struggle forward beyond her usual endurance. Her mind was filled by the oppressing weight of her losses.

I must keep going, she told herself. I can't stop. I won't quit. I just have to keep moving onward. I have to keep doing something to keep my mind occupied. If I stop and have too much time to think, I know I'll think only of Black Fox. I also have an enemy behind me. He will be following me. If I get far enough ahead of him, maybe I'll be able to check my back trail. For the present time, I just have to keep moving. I'll walk to the caves then the swamp. Black Fox said the swamp was a spiritual place for refuge. I need such a location now. I'll get rid o' my enemy in the swamp. Afterward, I'll go home. Maybe I can continue to enjoy catching fish and collecting rice in our valley. Some rice is stored in the rock bins. I have rabbit meat in the toboggan along with a little caribou meat.

Night Star enjoyed the familiar, whispering sound of her snowshoes moving across the snow. She kept walking steadily, pulling the toboggan behind her. The forest strangely seems to be the same, she reflected. I suppose, because my life has changed, I thought everything else would also change. The only thing apparently altered now is my view of life. The more I walk, and watch the land, I know that normal life will return to me through time.

Increasing sunlight, of a new day, lit her path among tall pines, beeches, oaks and maples. I have a companion that no enemy can take from me, she exclaimed defiantly to herself when she came to a particularly majestic area of beech trees and maples. Gray and dark trunks extended up to a canopy of branches silhouetted against a crystal, blue sky. Sunlight dropping through this canopy etched a network of shadowy patterns on the snow. With sunlight warming her, she thought, I have my family to the north in our valley beside the river. I will return to our winter camp. I must, however, get rid of my enemy before I go to my camp. I also have the forest with me. I have always been at home in the forest and, particularly, the swamp. An enemy follows me. However, I know my home.

With warming light around her, Night Star looked upward toward the sun and saw a thunderbird, the eagle. To the Great Spirit, she whispered, "Please stay with me and direct my path."

She heard a reply, saying, "Your friend has missed you." Without thinking, she asked herself, what friend do I have? She felt foolish when she realized her friend was the Great Spirit. Her friends were also her family to the north along with the forest and, particularly, the swamp. Moreover, she thought, I will, in my spirit life, again meet Black Fox.

Feeling comforted by knowing she wasn't alone, she gathered dry firewood and made a smokeless fire. She removed a rabbit from her snare bag and spitted this meat over the flames. She found the food to be nourishing and her strength revived. She boiled water in a small pottery bowl and prepared rice tea.

The tea and roasted meat helped to fill some of the empty feeling she had in her heart following the loss of Black Fox. Flames from the fire helped to dispel the cold feeling that also gnawed at her. She rested beside her fire then slept until red light of dawn filled the forest.

An hawk screamed from above the treetops. Night Star prepared her equipment for more traveling. I must stay well ahead of my enemy, she warned herself. I will first carry out Black Fox's plan of going to the caves. Afterward, I'll use my snare thong to snare my enemy at the spring in the swamp. I will use the thin ice above the spring to get rid of my enemy who has a twisted, painted face. I sense the presence of the Great Spirit in the forest. This part of the woods is particularly beautiful. These great trees belong to and are part of the Great Spirit. All trees are the same and so are the creatures of the forest including the swamp. Using additional rice, Night Star prepared more tea and slowly chewed the remaining, roasted, rabbit meat. I could circle back and follow my enemy in the manner of the grizzly bears of the forest and from our legends, she thought. I could also walk directly along my old trail and attack him. However, I think I'll snare my enemy. I know how to make and set snares, she said to herself while she checked her snares. She tied most of her snares together before she cut extra cord and added it to the others to make one very long thin, yet strong, line. To catch larger game, I simply need a bigger snare. To the top of the bundles of equipment on her toboggan, she tied her bow along with the quiver of arrows and the long, snare line.

Satisfied with her work and preparations, she started pulling the toboggan and walked westward. When an hawk screamed beyond the treetops, she stopped and said to herself, I would first like to know if an enemy follows me. Maybe I'll walk back in a wide circle and check my own trail to see if my danger is real or imagined. Maybe my enemy just went back home although I sense I am being followed. I want to make sure I have an enemy following my tracks before I risk going close to the spring.

When Night Star arrived at a creek flowing between snow-drifted banks, she walked down the bank and slowly drank some icy water. Deer prints accompanied by wolf tracks marked the snow-covered banks.

After drinking slowly because the water was so cold, she looked up along the banks and saw a deer standing among a section of maple saplings. The deer continued to stand and watch while Night Star untied her bow and quiver of arrows. She fitted an arrow to the bow's string and turned slowly before pulling back the string. She released the arrow, sending it arcing up and slightly over then down to the deer. The animal jumped forward and fell into the creek. Legs thrashed in blood stained water. These movements became slower until only the water stirred.

Night Star pulled her toboggan closer to the deer. Working quickly, she prepared the hide, meat bones and sinew. In an adjacent stand of cedars, where deer had been sleeping, she built a smokeless fire and skewered a stick through venison. This meat was held above the flames by a supporting, forked stick. A tantalizing fragrance of roasting venison drifted within a wall of surrounding cedars. After heating stones obtained from the streambed, she placed them in water contained in a watertight, birch bark basket. The water heated rapidly. Next she added rice grains to the boiling water and prepared rice tea to accompany the juicy and flavorful venison.

With roasted venison and rice tea reviving her strength, and giving her some comfort, Night Star rested. She started to look at her world differently. Her customary assurance started to return. While flames of the fire provided warmth and light, her thoughts stirred with usual clarity and strength. I don't think I'll check to see if an enemy is following me because he might turn on to my fresh tracks and catch me. I'll set a snare for him them watch to see if he gets caught. This enemy is likely not a better traveler than a deer and I can wear out a deer on a trail. I would avoid a fight if I could. I wouldn't deliberately harm anyone. However, I must get rid of this enemy before I return to my northern valley because, if I bring an enemy home, he would harm my village. I'll make sure I'm not being followed then I can go to my valley. I miss my winter camp beside the river. I have meat on my toboggan. There is some rice in the stone, storage bins. I enjoy living in the valley where there is shelter from the wind. The river provides water along with fish and I will try to return to my normal life.

Night Star made no effort to hide her tracks when she left the camp and started pulling the toboggan behind her. She resumed her journey through a forest of tall trees. Her snowshoes whispered across a layer of powdery snow on top of an older, icy crust. She proceeded westward under branches of towering, white pines, hemlocks, elms, maples and birches. A breeze whirred among lofty boughs.

My toboggan leaves a clear trail anyone could follow, she said to herself. I won't try to hide such a path. I'll use it to snare my enemy with the twisted face. I have a plan and I'll stick to it. When I'm sure I'm right, I don't change my mind. I've been snaring animals all my life in order to get food along with furs. I'm sure I can snare this man who follows me. Maybe he will get tired and go home. If he keeps pursuing me, he will get caught in one of my snares.

Night Star walked in a golden haze of sunlight spreading among tree branches and trunks. She held the stone carving of the Arctic owl, or thunderbird, in her hand and felt she was being kindly watched by the Great Spirit. The man tracking me, thought Night Star, must be wondering whom he is following. He must be expecting me to tire soon. He should leave me alone and save his own life.

Night Star was reassured when she saw, on the pine branch, a thunderbird, the Arctic owl. These messengers of the Great Spirit know I'm in trouble and will remind the

Great Spirit of my distress, she said to herself.

Chewing roasted venison to get strength, Night Star kept walking until she faced a pink sky above the setting sun. The horizon darkened gradually then she traveled across a pale sheen of moonlight on the snow. Moonlight became brighter and hit a distant peak of high rocks. She proceeded onward and reached elevated terrain where a cliff was silhouetted against a background of a darker sky. A shadow flickered across snow beside her when a broad winged owl flew overhead.

Feeling comforted by the owl's company, Night Star slept beside her toboggan. She slept fitfully because of the cold.

In order to get warm, she started walking again, crossing intricate patterns of moonlight and shadows on the snow. Deer trails accompanied by wolf tracks marked the snow. Wolves howled in the distance. An owl hooted repeatedly. The wolf howls and owl calls rang clearly through the crisp air.

She kept climbing to higher terrain, helped by the gray light of dawn. Shafts of sunlight, from the eastern horizon, painted clouds with hues of gold and red. When Night Star approached the rocks that stand up, they were etched in gold against a backdrop of ragged, amber clouds. She followed a well-used porcupine path to large, broken rocks beneath the standing rocks. The path led inside the cliff.

The trail became too narrow for the toboggan to be pulled through easily. Night Star hid it, together with other bulky equipment, among some boulders. Here too, she left her snowshoes. Leaving most of her equipment behind, she continued following the path until it came to a dark opening in the cliff. At the entrance to this cave, there were mounds of porcupine droppings. She stepped inside the first of an apparent series of darkened rooms. The cliff seems to have broken and now the two sides lean against each other, she said to herself. Light enters from overhead openings.

In the first chamber, there was an old fireplace in the center of the floor. The second room was the same. On a shelf, at the far end of the second cavern, there was a cluster of flint, spear points along with a flint knife. The third cave had the same central fire pit.

Night Star trembled as legends sprang to life in her mind when she looked at the north wall of the third cave. On this surface, chipped in the stone, there was a drawing of a great grizzly. The first people to live here saw a world that we see no more, she thought. We still have grizzlies on our land although they must not be as large as the legendary bears.

On the west wall, there was a narrow break. Looking into this opening, Night Star saw another cave. She entered the opening. Her leather clothing, and tomahawk in her belt, scraped against the stone walls when she squeezed through the passageway. The cave was long and narrow. She walked down a path descending beside an ice flow resembling a frozen creek. The cave people must've stored food here, she thought while staring at this place where many people had lived a long time in the past. The air was cold and damp.

I came here due to respect for Black Fox, reflected Night Star. He wanted to see these caves. In spirit, maybe he is with me. I am pleased I visited this place. Now I have to leave. I must escape.

A grating sound, of stone and leather scraping against the passageway's walls, sent a chill of fear tingling through her. Terror gripped her stomach. Remaining completely still, she watched the narrow, dimly lit entranceway. Was my enemy always closer than I thought? Night Star asked herself. Has he waited to trap me here?

While fear continued to trickle through her, leaving her tense, she checked her flint knife then her tomahawk. Leaving the knife in her belt, she held the tomahawk in her left hand and also gathered, in her left hand, some smooth stones. I have to fight my own way, she thought. I use snares. I also throw stones to get birds and rabbits for food. Maybe stones will now protect me from this enemy. Can he hear my heart pounding? My throat is dry.

She waited. Hearing no further sounds, she started climbing upward toward the passageway.

The entrance is narrow, she thought. My enemy will be confident because he has trapped me. Maybe he has trapped himself in a narrow passageway. Almost frantically, she picked up more stones, placing them together on the cave's floor.

She resolved to act rather than wait to be attacked. Selecting a particularly round stone, she threw it with all her force and previously honed skill. Before the first rock hit the passageway's walls, the second stone was in the air. Other rocks followed in rapid succession. An anguished scream answered the ricocheting of rocks from one wall to another along the crevasse. A short groan followed the scream. Tomahawk in hand, Night Star ran swiftly to the narrow opening. She kept running and jumped passed the bent form of Winter Hawk.

Seizing her chance to escape, she fled through the caves and reached her toboggan. She slipped on her snowshoes, pulled her toboggan and, with each step, she joyously got farther away from the crouched form in the passageway. In order to walk as rapidly as possible, she followed her old, snowshoe prints topped by the tracks of her enemy with the twisted face. She kept traveling until exhaustion forced her to rest. Looking back along her trail, she saw no movements and heard no sounds indicating she was being followed. She pushed onward and lengthening shadows found her camped in a secluded site surrounded by cedars.

Warmed by a small fire, she cooked a last piece of caribou meat she had almost forgotten about. She also steeped rice to make tea. The snow-covered forest received a pink hue from a red sunset. Distant cave cliffs were silhouetted against a red sky. Before red light had completely faded, Night Star saw a broad-winged, Arctic owl fly to a cedar next to the toboggan trail from the caves. The owl will warn me if the enemy approaches, Night Star thought before sipping her favorite drink of rice tea. So far, there has been no sign of that man. Possibly I seriously injured him and now he will leave. I could've killed him; yet all I could think about was escaping. If he keeps following me, I'll snare him in the swamp then I'll go home. I went to the caves to carry out Black Fox's dream of seeing the old place where people lived a long time ago. If the owl flies up in fright, I'll know I am again being followed.

Stars brightened the sky. Gradually, an amber moon appeared

above the eastern horizon and formed shadows on the snow-covered, forest's floor.

Night Star woke up and was placing wood on her fire when she saw the owl swoop down from the cedar. The broad-winged hunter caught a rabbit and took it back to the cedar. Almost immediately, the owl left the cedar. The large bird dropped the rabbit during an hasty flight eastward.

The frightened owl dropped the rabbit, said Night Star to herself. Something scared the bird and my old enemy follows me. Packing her equipment rapidly, she started pulling the toboggan behind her, resuming her journey to the east.

My enemy knows now that I'm not an easy catch, reasoned Night Star while her snowshoes carried her forward in a reassuring rhythm. He also knows I leave an easy trail to follow. Anyone could follow the toboggan's path along the snow. He must have confirmed that my advantage lies not in hiding my tracks but by traveling with speed and strength. I can use the knowledge he has of me to defeat him.

Moonlight, shining among towering trees, brightened the forest. During Night Star's journey, she started to enjoy again the endless beauty of the world as it had been created by the Great Spirit. How intriguing are the Great Spirit's thoughts of beauty when the world was made, she reflected. We were all made together; yet some people move away from the Creator and this causes trouble we call evil. Such an evil one who walks away from the Creator follows me. I'll snare him and send him back to the spirit world where he will see the error and evil of his ways. He follows me at his own peril. He pursues me to the swamp. I feel I am at home there and am closer to my great friend. Evil is the moving away from my friend. I know that feeling and don't like it. It brings a cold, empty sensation. Real power rests with the Great Spirit who experiences and enjoys life through works of creation. I think the purpose of life is to experience living and stay with the Creator rather than moving away. Moving away brings trouble. The Great Spirit is actually in works of creation such as the forest. Such spiritual presence protects the land. Trees don't have a choice of moving closer to or farther away from the Creator. People can decide to move closer to the Great Spirit or withdraw more. I seek and have asked to remain closer and that helps me to feel secure even during a time of being pursued.

Night Star enjoyed the crisp, bright cleanness of the land. Occasionally, from a lofty tree, an owl hooted. Wolves howled. The forest was a living and active world.

In a dense grove of cedars, Night Star risked starting a small fire. She cooked a rabbit and prepared rice tea. Following this meal, she rested and noted the intricate patterns formed upon the snow by moonlight glowing among tree trunks and branches. Fatigue helped her to sleep.

Night Star woke up when a shrill cry of an hawk rang through the forest. The morning was particularly cold. Flakes of snow shimmered through sunlight dropping in wedges from breaks in scattered clouds. Instantly worried about having lost time, she quickly packed her equipment on her toboggan and started pulling it behind her. When she pushed onward, her snowshoes whispered across a light, powdery layer of fresh snow. Stopping seldom, she walked steadily through the forest.

She tried to stop to sleep but sleep would not come to her although this interval allowed her to rest. She prepared tea and chewed some previously roasted, rabbit meat.

Late afternoon sunlight was outlining clouds with red tints when Night Star approached Spirit Swamp. Close to the swamp, she came upon large tracks in the snow. Grizzly bears usually sleep during the winter, she said to herself while following the worrisomely large prints. Grizzlies are not as large now as the great bears of the past and those from legends like the drawing in the cave. These tracks are from the smaller, hump-backed bears we see today. I have much respect for such creatures. I hope this resident of the swamp won't bother me.

Night Star continued following the bear's tracks. They led her to a dense stand of cedars and hemlocks. She circled this thicket of trees until she saw the bear tracks coming out from the other side. After making certain the bear had left the area, she stepped among the cedars and hemlocks. An encircling wall of trees left an interior space well suited for a camp.

Welcoming the solitude provided by a surrounding wall of branches and trunks, she quickly prepared a comfortable home. She sat down on a ledge with a warming fire flickering in front of her. From this comfortable location, she roasted venison by skewering a stick through a chunk of meat and holding it above the flames.

She enjoyed the appearance of security established by closely intermingled branches. Flames flickered light across the surrounding greenery. The sky turned crimson before darkening then fading before the moon appeared and brightened the snow-cloaked woods.

Night Star slept beside her fire. She was awakened by the crunching and snow-squeaking sounds of something, or someone, walking toward her camp. The sounds became clearer as the intruder came closer. She fitted an arrow to the string of her bow. She also placed a spear beside her. She feared that any, or every, enemy would be able to hear her heart pounding in the still solitude of the night. My enemy has caught up to me, she said to herself. Could it be the bear?

Branches shook before parting to reveal a massive, advancing head of a grizzly. Jaws opened, spewing out a loud, menacing growl. After releasing this blast, the head shook from side to side. Dark eyes stared at Night Star then the creature turned around to move again through the wall of branches. They fell back into place, leaving Night Star watching her enclosed camp lit by a flame curling above embers. Crunching, snow-squeaking sounds, beyond the enclosure, were at first loud and clear. They faded gradually until only silence stalked the land.

Did the great bear turn away because it wished me no harm? Night Star asked herself before placing wood on the fire. Or did the Great Spirit protect me? I will always bet on the Great Spirit.

From a leather bag on her toboggan, she removed a small, blackened, pottery bowl. It was finely decorated with lines in the clay in addition to a symbol of a thunderbird. She removed her necklace containing the stone thunderbird and placed it in the bowl. She sank the bowl in earth softened by the fire's warmth on the eastern side of the fire. "Thank you, Great Spirit, for protecting me," she whispered.

The gray light of dawn added distinct outlines to trees. Realizing that morning was upon her, Night Star prepared her equipment and left the camp. Pulling the toboggan behind her, she followed the bear tracks. They provided a clear trail heading toward the large, ice-and-snow-covered pond formed by the spring.

These bear tracks might save my life, exclaimed Night Star to herself as she walked beside the large, deep prints winding toward the pond. Any ice strong enough to support a bear's weight will also support me. I wonder if the bear would know or could detect that the pond's ice is unsafe above the spring. Black Fox warned me to stay away from the western side of the pond because, in that area, water bubbles out of a deep, hole in the clay. Moving water prevents ice from forming securely above the spring. Black Fox said he learned much about the spring from his father, White Stone. He had been chasing a caribou. In a desperate attempt to escape, the caribou had crossed the pond and fallen through thin ice above the spring.

Night Star continued walking beside the bear's tracks. They led her to the western part of the pond and then vanished. Beyond the last track, there were no marks in snow covering ice above the area where the spring was located. That's the strangest thing I've seen in a while, she thought. If the animal had fallen through the ice, there would be a watery section ahead of the tracks. However, the bear prints lead only to unmarked snow covering ice above the spring. The prints don't turn to one side or another. The bear could only have turned around and walked back along its own prints. I didn't notice the change because I was looking too far ahead and thinking about other things.

Looking more carefully at the snow covering the pond, at the place where the spring was supposed to be, she noticed a slight, dark, blue line of wet snow slanting to the northwest. After checking the grizzly's tracks again, Night Star realized the bear had turned back along its own trail before veering directly southward. The animal smelled water, or sensed danger some other way, and abruptly headed south, reasoned Night Star. The critter has led me as far as I can safely travel along the ice on this pond. I have to act quickly.

Working rapidly and skillfully, following years of experience with snares, Night Star assembled most of her snares in addition to fish lines and extra cords. She tied all these pieces together, forming a long cord coiled neatly in front of her on the snow. She tied the bottom end of the cord to her toboggan. The top part of this cord was then tied behind the tip of an arrow she fitted to the string of her bow. With a skilled motion, she pulled the arrow back to its full length in the bow. When the arrow was released, it shot skyward, passing over the spring and pulling line away from coils in front of the toboggan. The arrow dropped on the far side of the pond. The cord, tied to this arrow, stretched across the spring and remained fastened to the toboggan.

Night Star removed her snowshoes and carried them, temporarily abandoning her toboggan along with its equipment. She carefully stepped into the bear's prints and followed them southward. By concealing her moccasin prints inside the grizzly tracks, she walked through the forest until she was far enough away from the pond to be able to slip her feet back into her snowshoes. She traveled northward so she could get to the far side of the ice-covered pond and retrieve her arrow.

Picking up her arrow, she untied it then returned it to her quiver on her back. Next she grasped the line and started pulling it. She slowly hauled in line and dragged the toboggan toward her, extending its trail over thin ice above the spring. The toboggan crossed the blue slash of wet snow and came to Night Star. She looked backward along the toboggan's unbroken trail crossing the snow on thin ice above the spring.

After fastening her bow and quiver of arrows to the toboggan, she continued walking northward, leaving behind a clearly marked toboggan path in the snow.

Having traveled northeastward across flat terrain, she turned directly northward and proceeded toward an high, long hill. She climbed this hill and followed its summit until she located a place providing an unobstructed view of her back trail. Night Star sat down and rested. From this site, on the high stretch of land, she looked back and could see the path of her toboggan winding through the swamp and crossing the snow-and-ice-covered pond above the hidden spring.

Night Star waited with the patience of a skilled hunter. I have to wait now, she reminded herself. I don't want to go home with an enemy following me because such a person would injure anyone at my winter camp or village. I'll snare him first before I return to my sheltered valley with the stone caches beside the Shebeshekong River. The riverbanks are fine places for my snares. I can also get fish and sometimes shoot deer or moose. We usually collect much rice before winter arrives. The river provides a winter home for me. I long to return to my camp. However, I must make sure I don't have an enemy pursuing me before I resume my journey to the north.

She waited until the sun dipped below the western horizon, spraying clouds with scarlet shafts of light. Scarlet hues deepened to become crimson before fading and becoming lost among night's shadows. Remaining light came from pale snow tinted red by the first appearance of the moon glimmering among trunks and branches.

On the hill, close to Night Star's resting place, there was a well-used wolf trail. It joined places of trampled snow where wolves had also waited and watched the southern landscape. When the snow melts, the wolves have their dens on the south, or sunlit, side of this hill, observed Night Star. Black Fox often mentioned the wolf dens on this hillside. According to the trails, the wolves also use this place as a lookout point during other seasons such as winter.

Close to Night Star's position, beyond trees and brush, a wolf howled. The call was a long, plaintive voice that seemed to encompass and express the forest itself. A paling moon appeared to disentangle itself from treetops then ascend into a starlit sky.

I've been setting snares all my life, reflected Night Star. I like rabbits although I have to trap them for food. I wouldn't do any unnecessary harm to them or anything else. I prefer to not harm my enemy. I would be pleased if he would just stop following me. I'll snare him only to protect myself just the way I catch rabbits to get food and not because I want to hurt them. I wouldn't harm anything unnecessarily. My enemy has the choice of walking away and not following me. I don't have a choice because I must defend myself. His evil intentions for me drive him onward. The evil he plans for me will actually come to him. I don't understand why people are attracted to destructive plans. Such individuals usually don't discover soon enough that people who plan trouble also bring as much, or more, harm to themselves. I have asked for the Great Spirit's help and guidance. If my enemy's mind is set for destruction, then hopefully my toboggan's path will lead him to nothing more than the harm he intends for me.

As if connected to Night Star's thoughts regarding her enemy, something appeared to be moving at the end of the trail she was watching. Like a spider checking its web, she focused her attention of the distant object advancing along the toboggan's path.

If this moving thing is an animal, thought Night Star, it might ruin my trail. After the thing had advanced closer to the pond, she said to herself with a mixture of worry and excitement, there is no animal tracking me. Along my trail, walks a person and this person is my enemy.

Fascinated, while being gripped by both fear and excitement, she observed her toboggan trail and her enemy followed this path toward the pond. He didn't alter his stride in any way. He appeared to look neither to one side or the other. He continued onward, using a distance eating rhythm of walking that brought him onto the pond.

Night Star's heart pounded. She viewed her trail with concern, knowing any twist or turn of a rabbit can leave an empty snare.

This enemy, however, clearly seemed to have taken the bait and was pursuing the trail of the toboggan pulled by a cord across the snow-and-ice-covered pond. Will he notice the absence of my snowshoe prints that often remain partially hidden under the toboggan's path? Night Star asked herself. Maybe the ice above the spring is strong enough to hold this person and I will be the one getting snared in my own trap.

The man kept advancing with an unaltered pace then dropped out of sight. Night Star thought she might have heard a yell or a crash of breaking ice. She saw his arms flail in the air as his body went through the ice over the spring. His arms thrashed against the ice before slowly descending out of view, leaving behind a dark stain of water on the pale, snowy surface of the pond marked by a toboggan's trail.

Continuing to look toward the pond, Night Star saw no further movements. Silence and stillness stalked the swamp where, previously, there had been a moving enemy. She felt tension dissolve from her head. She was greatly relieved to have escaped from the enemy following her and also the worry that had been in her mind. Her world started returning to normal again, allowing her to enjoy the pleasure and comfort of being alive without the pain of worry.

An eerie, tingling sensation trickled through her mind when she considered her changed situation. Although she found no joy in her enemy's destruction, it gave her freedom to return to normal activities. She had received another chance for life and, through this second opportunity, she felt the presence and guidance of the Great Spirit. Never again, for the remainder of my life, she resolved, will I overlook the caring guidance of my friend, the Great Spirit whose presence I particularly notice in this swamp. The swamp is a special place that is protected so creatures and people can come here for renewal. An elder told me that only rocks live forever. I now know this elder was mistaken because only the spirit world of the Creator lives forever. This world's birds, trees, rocks and people, all live forever as part of the Great Spirit. Special places, like this swamp, protect animals and bring awareness to people in order that they can get closer to the spirit. Spiritual closeness gives happiness to a person just as distance causes problems. We are never alone. Sometimes we think we are alone and such thoughts bring desperation. I appear to be traveling alone at the present time although I actually have the companionship and guidance of the Great Spirit.

A shadow flickered across the snow in front of Night Star. Looking up, she saw an Arctic owl. This hunter was flying overhead in a sky becoming pale in the first light of dawn. I thought I was here only a short time, thought Night Star. I can't believe I've been watching the swamp all night.

Working quickly, she prepared the toboggan for traveling. Pulling it behind her, she started walking northward toward her other home beside the river in the valley. My home includes the river with its valley and the stone caches, she said to herself. My life includes the trees and hills with the birds, plants, fish, animals and people. I particularly feel I have come home when I visit this swamp. In such a place, I am more aware of the presence of the Great Spirit who works through the woods to move one person here and another there to give each one the arranged opportunity to have the best of life. Like the birds and animals, I have been protected and renewed in the swamp. Now I walk out from the swamp and carry awareness of the spirit with me to the valley of the river.

THREE

SPIRIT SWAMP

1645

Maybe I have made another mistake, Randin Blake told himself when he steered his heavily loaded trade canoe out of the river and into its tributary. The other traders said this journey would be my last. If this might be my last tradin' trip, I must appreciate each day and, if I'm careful, I might add extra days. I'll enjoy each day as if it might be my last chance to see the woods. If I have only a few days remaining, I couldn't pick a place to visit that's better than the legendary Spirit Swamp. I have just left the Pine River and, if I understand my directions correctly, I've entered the Willow River. I'll have to watch for Spring Creek because it flows out of the swamp. The other traders warned me that peace would not last. They think the Algonkians and Hurons of this region will again join with the French to go to war against the English traders, like myself, along with the Dutch traders and the

Iroquois. The English and Iroquois are strong allies; yet I am alone here in the land of the Algonkians and Hurons. The Iroquois, south o' here, are running short o' beaver and are trying to expand their trading empire northward. Since I'm one of the English traders who trade with the Iroquois, I thought I'd head north and see what this northern area was like. We are at peace now, so I took this chance to see this northern territory. The Hurons hunt here and so do the Ojibway. The Ojibway are one of the Algonkian nations, allied with the Hurons and French against the English and Iroquois. The French don't want the Algonkian and Huron trade to go south to the Iroquois and then to the Dutch and English. My trading partners think this peace will fail and I'll find myself in the middle of a new war. They say an English trader will not be welcome in the land of the Algonkians, Hurons or French. However, I'm a fur trader and the beaver furs are in the northwest. I have traveled into hostile territory to do my work. Why should I stay where the beaver furs dwindle each year? The center of the trade has moved northwest. I have to move with the work. No one agreed with me. No one would come with me. If I am wrong, I'll be the only one to suffer for my mistake. If I am right, I will share the results.

Rand was distracted from his thoughts when a beaver swam away from the far bank and started crossing in front of the canoe. Getting too close to the canoe, the beaver slammed its tail against the water, sending up a plume of spray before slipping under the river's surface. Farther downstream, the beaver reappeared only to slam its tail against the surface again and vanish under outward expanding ripples.

Turning a corner in the river, Randin saw a moose standing close to the bank. Rand decided to risk a shot and raised his musket. He sighted quickly at a point just behind the animal's front leg. The sound of the shot blasted through the forest and the moose fell forward into the stream. Legs flailed briefly then all movements ceased. Water swirled around the bulky form.

Rand paddled his canoe to the bank. After stepping into shallow water, he used a piece of rawhide cord to tie his craft to a tree's trunk. Working quickly with his skinning knife, he removed the hide. It was placed in the canoe and functioned as a carrying bag for large quantities of meat. Other meat was carried up a rocky slope to a camping place. He labored at preparing his meat supply and camp until evening's shadows enveloped the woods except for the area brightened by a flickering campfire.

Rand washed in the river. He was a muscular man of medium height with dark eyes. His black, gray-flecked hair was long, matching his beard.

He was intrigued by the pattern of shadows across the river. He was watching these forms when some of them merged into the outline of a moose. This animal walked in shallow water beside the opposite bank and gradually rejoined other shapes to become lost from view in the murkiness of night.

Upright, forked stakes supported poles slanted above the flames. Chunks of roasting moose meat were skewered on the sharpened poles. Emitting delicious aromas, the meat sizzled and dropped oil into the brightly flickering flames.

Rand cut off a wedge of cooked meat. He added salt and pepper to this morsel before placing it in his mouth and chewing it slowly. The food was warm, tender, juicy and filled with a mild, smoky flavor. He savored additional chunks until the skewers were empty. Afterward, he sipped tea and rested. He kept his fire small, feeding it often to keep a steady flame brightening the camp.

Upon lighting his pipe, he said to himself, I know the Ojibway hunters come here. They are also called Algonkians and speak the Algonkian language. Huron hunters visit this swamp. They speak the Iroquoian language although they are allied with the Algonkians along with the French and are enemies of the Iroquois Confederacy and the English. The hunters, traders or trappers I might meet here could all be my enemies. I must be careful. I'll make the most of each day although I think I've done that all my life.

Something large growled close to Rand's camp. A bear, he told himself as he reached for his musket. I don't like havin' bears around at night because I can't see them well enough.

A black bear cub came into view just where firelight was mixing with shadows at the edge of camp. A second cub moved in pale moonlight in front of boulders. Looming largely among these same rocks, there was the form of an adult bear. She was sitting down and watching her cubs.

I don't want the cubs to come into my camp, Rand told himself. The mother bear might think she has to protect them and attack me.

The eyes of the closest cub sparkled in firelight. Although distrustful of lurking, human scent, the young bear approached Rand until a wisp of smoke drifted to the bear's nostrils. Sniffing this smoke, the animal sprang back and scrambled toward the other cub. Both young bears ran to the adult and she ambled through shadows, quickly moving out of view. They've gone, fortunately, Rand said to himself.

Randin emptied his canoe. He turned his craft on its side with the interior facing the fire. Under this shelter, he placed his equipment and stretched a bear hide on the ground for protection from the cold earth and stones. Sitting down on the makeshift bed, he used a stick from the fire to light his pipe again. He enjoyed the fragrance of burning tobacco. The night was generally quiet. Occasionally a twig snapped or a branch cracked. Frogs croaked resonantly. An owl hooted. Wolves howled from the northwest. The sky sparkled with stars and the moon added light to the forest. An heron croaked while flying overhead. A large flock of honking geese circled above the swamp and Rand could see their dark forms passing across the silver moon. This swamp is part of me, reflected Rand. There's a spirit here and the spirit of this forest is my friend. I'm at home here and wish no harm to anything although I have to hunt to eat and I'm a fur trader. The world is a strange place because my only actual enemies are other people.

Rand noted each sound and movement in the forest. His camp was sheltered from the prevailing, west wind. The only sound I haven't heard here yet is the call of a whippoorwill, observed Rand while he watched a tendril of smoke from his pipe twist eastward, carried away by a fitful breeze rustling among branches. The call of a whippoorwill is one of my favorite forest sounds along with an howl of a wolf, call of a loon and song of a robin or cardinal. I'm also always fascinated by the resonant honking of geese during their flights above the forest.

Rand prepared tea and sipped it contentedly. At the present time, the Hurons, Algonkians and French are at peace with the Iroquois and their trading partners, the Dutch and English, Rand recalled. The English will take over from the Dutch in the fur trade with the Iroquois. If the Iroquois can trade northward with the Hurons along with Algonkian nations, such as the Ojibway, then a new flow of furs can replace the dwindling supply in the southern region. The Hurons and Ojibway would win regardless of whether their furs went east to the French or south to the English and Iroquois. However, the French won't agree to a southern branch to the fur trade. If furs aren't allowed to go south then there will be more war. Because beavers are getting scarce in the south, the Iroquois and English, including traders such as myself, are going to be moving northward to get more furs. Conflict should be unnecessary because the land is large enough for each trader to get furs. I'll see how welcome an English trader will be in this northern region. There is peace in the woods at the present time although, likely, peace won't last. I have a plan to go where the trading is best. We have to expand in order to compete. Maybe life has always been this way. We have to expand northward into the trading territory of our recent enemies, the Hurons, Algonkians and French. Maybe my trip northward will help my other English and Iroquois traders. I like to work and be busy. I have to try to do my best work. The largest failure is not trying. The present peace between the two trading alliances has given me an opportunity to travel northward and I have to take this chance. I'll trap for furs, do some trading and get information about the northern trade before I return to the south. This land seems to have enough furs for all the trappers and traders.

Across the river, where firelight lost itself among shadows, there loomed an outline of a moose. Stepping into the water, the bull raised its head, sniffed the air and turned around to step among alders. Diminishing sounds of snapping twigs and branches marked the route the animal took as it walked away from the unwelcome, human scent.

Upstream, a beaver slammed its tail against the river's surface, sending up a white plume of spray. From this same area, a long, plaintive howl of a wolf spoke to the first light of dawn.

The forest brightened slowly under a gray sky. The river was calm although a restless, west wind stirred treetops. Randin Blake added wood to his fire before he skewered chunks of moose meat on sticks supported above the flames. After enjoying a meal of juicy, tender meat, he constructed a drying rack above the fire and smoked a large supply of meat.

He finished butchering the moose. He carried unused portions away from camp and left this food for other creatures in the woods. I never waste anything, he said to himself after turning slabs of meat on the drying rack. I also believe in sharing everything.

While Rand watched the river, he often noticed large fins breaking through the water's surface. He cut down a black, spruce sapling and trimmed away the branches in addition to sharpening one end to make a fishing spear. The next time a fin broke through the river's surface, he thrust his spear under this target. The sharpened point stuck into the body of a large, fighting salmon. Mustering his strength, Rand pushed the shaft upward, keeping its point imbedded in the struggling fish. With an arcing swirl of blood, the salmon fell off the spear and dropped onto the riverbank. Rand continued spearing fish until he had a large number of salmon piled beside the drying rack.

I'm going to winter well this year, he thought before adding slabs of salmon meat to the drying rack. I'm going to have lots o' food. I'll move away from the river and build a cabin. I'm already enjoying the north woods. There are many beavers in this swamp. I have started a great journey. I made the right decision when I decided to risk everything and travel north to the legendary, hunting ground called Spirit Swamp. I'll cache much of my food. Afterward, I will build a cabin nearby so I can come here and get the stored food.

I make my own plans, thought Randin when he pushed his loaded canoe into the Willow River. The other traders said I shouldn't go north because peace won't last between the two, trading alliances. I traveled north anyway and have found that I was right. I've accomplished the task of designing my own plan then carrying it out successfully. I have entered a paradise in this swamp. It's full of game and has much fur. I can trap beavers and maybe trade for more furs before I return to the south, hauling a rich cargo of furs. I'm enjoying this swamp. I feel like I belong here. I was right to travel northward.

The calm, river's surface mirrored surrounding banks, trees and sky. The canoe cut across, and sent ripples moving under, a reflection of the forest. Ravens croaked from a gray sky. A vulture circled tirelessly overhead.

Paddling his canoe against the first beaver dam, he climbed over bundles of equipment and stepped onto the low dam. On top of this barricade, the beavers had added fresh cuttings of poplar in addition to a few stones. Beaver tracks were marked in the mud. These tracks were combined with some large, wolf prints.

Rand unloaded packs before hauling his craft across the dam. The canoe slipped through fresh mud and entered water below the obstacle. Avoiding a torrent of water escaping from an opening between poles, he replaced his packs. He also had to unload his canoe before taking it across other low dams. Often, by paddling swiftly, he was able to rush his craft across the lowest dams slightly protruding from the surface.

He steered the canoe into the swiftest part of the current while guiding the bark sides away from rocks or logs. Although he always tried to protect his canoe, it started to leak. When he noticed water on the floor of his craft, he stopped in front of an area where the river was forced to flow more swiftly between two outcroppings of smooth rocks.

He nudged the bark side of the canoe against the rocky bank then stepped onto the rocks. After unloading his packs, he prepared a camp, using his canoe as a shelter.

He located a break in one of the seams between two layers of bark on his canoe. To stop water from leaking through this break, he covered this section with a sticky mixture of heated, spruce gum and fat. Afterward, he enjoyed his camp and roasted salmon over the fire.

Upon steeping tea, he sipped it slowly before lighting his pipe. Maybe the people here are my enemies, he reflected as he watched the flames of his fire flickering brightly in front of a shadowy background of the river and forest. This land, however, is my friend. I'll build a cabin here and stay for the winter. There are lots o' beavers around and I can trap during the winter.

Rand slept comfortably on the bearskin. He was awakened at daybreak by honking calls from a flock of geese flying across a gray sky. The grayness of the dawn was reflected on the river's surface.

Using pieces of dry hemlock, he coaxed a flame out of embers in the fire pit. The fire brought welcome heat and light to the camp. Rand prepared a meal of roasted moose meat followed by tea.

He felt contented when he again pushed his canoe into the stream. I have journeyed into the territory of my enemies, he said to himself, and, so far, I've seen no sign of them. Even if I meet Ojibway or Huron hunters, and maybe a French trader, we are supposed to be at peace.

After placing packs in the canoe and erasing traces of his camping place, he stepped into his craft, sat down comfortably and was pleased to be floating again on the river, paddling downstream.

Having progressed slowly because he had to cross two, particularly large, dams, he reached the outlet of Spring Creek. He turned the bow of his canoe into this calm waterway. Evening shadows darkened much of the water although a rising moon provided murky light.

A beaver slammed its tail against the creek's surface, sending up a flash of spray. Maybe I'll do most of my traveling at night, thought Randin. I might encounter enemies in this legendary swamp.

The creek's surface became a path of silvery light winding between banks topped by aged willows and cedars. Higher sections of land contained hemlocks and maples with some beeches and white pines. These trees were duplicated in shadows patterning the silvery course of the creek. Beaver lodges were regularly spaced among low dams that the canoe could push across without getting caught.

The land was flat and swampy although the water was fresh and clean. Ducks quacked from other watery places in the swamp. An owl hooted occasionally. Wolves howled farther to the north.

Randin Blake felt he was part of the land and, having such an attitude, he thought this swamp was his home although it was considered to be in the territory of a possibly hostile alliance of nations. When he heard the barking, he, at first, thought the wolves were coming closer. The barking continued without accompanying howls. Wolves usually don't bark that way, Rand warned himself. A dog is barking ahead of me. I must be approaching some people. They are likely Ojibway, Huron or French, so I'll have to be cautious. Fortunately, I feel at home in this swamp although I have human enemies. My canoe passing through here is as natural as a leaf drifting along the water's surface. I'm part of this swamp, like the beavers and trees.

Something hissed passed Randin's face and slammed into a tree's trunk on the south side of the creek. Struck by shock, he stopped paddling. Fear flashed through him when he realized the whizzing thing could have been an arrow. He crouched forward and started paddling furiously just before other shafts whirred passed him. A musket blasted from the north bank. Rand cried out, gripped his main supply pack and fell against the side of his canoe, overturning it. He stayed on the south side of his swamped canoe, keeping it, along with his floating packs, between him and arrows that whizzed around him. A musket fired again, kicking up a burst of spray. An arrow stuck in the special pack he was pushing in front of his face.

Leaving his canoe and packs drifting behind him, he continued using the main pack for buoyancy and protection while he swam upstream against the current. He moved behind gnarled, willow trunks then kept following the creek.

He crawled behind a trunk and waited. Hearing splashing sounds downstream, he thought, they're collecting my supplies and canoe. As I go upstream, the water gets slightly cooler. I'm moving toward the spring. My enemies will think I'm dead, lying in the water. When they don't find my body, they might do a little searching in the chance I escaped from all the shooting. I must keep traveling quickly and silently.

Randin kept moving throughout the night. He hid among alders while men in two canoes paddled upstream. They returned silently, moving like shadows. The canoes were the only forms stirring in a generally still swamp. Fortunately I noticed them before they saw me, Rand said to himself.

After reaching the pond, he did not want to risk being seen on the large stretch of water. I must stay hidden, he warned himself. I'll remain among the willows and bulrushes. If I go southward, I can reach some higher ground and build a camp in order to get dry and warm. There's a lot o' clay along the creek's bed and on the bottom of this pond. Maybe the people I met came here to get clay for making pottery. I possibly disturbed a family and the barking dog warned them that I was approaching. I've lost my trading supplies although I have kept my main pack.

In the first, gray light of dawn, Rand was relieved to step out of the water. He walked among willows and decided to prepare a camp in an area of high ground hidden by hemlocks along with some birches and beeches.

He cut boughs to make a mattress on a ridge overlooking downward sloping ground where he built a fire. Above his mattress, he constructed a rough, lean-to topped by overlapping, hemlock boughs.

Constant work kept him warm. He washed his clothes at the far side of a pond in front of his camp. Wearing his long underwear, he hung his other clothing on an hide line near the fire. Lastly, he prepared tea. All my food was lost with my canoe and most of my other supplies, he said to himself. Fortunately, I always keep my main equipment beside me and I have it with me now. My enemies must think they shot me when I yelled and fell out of my canoe. They're probably now dividing my possessions. The enemy camp must be downstream where the dog barked. Maybe the dog barked earlier and I didn't hear it. The first barking would've warned my enemies of my approach. I guess the new peace doesn't extend to strangers or to English traders. I'll rest and get warm today. Tonight, I have to go downstream and see if I can reclaim my canoe. I must have a canoe. I could make one but peeling bark for a canoe is really only practical in the spring when the sap makes bark easier to peel without splitting. I'll try to recover a canoe tonight. If my attempt fails then I'll have to attempt to make a suitable craft.

Heat from the fire quickly dried Rand's clothes. He rested and absorbed warmth from the flames. He remained most of the time within the protective wall of hemlocks.

After sleeping occasionally, he prepared more tea and sipped it slowly. He also smoked his clay pipe while watching as much as he

could see of the swamp. More flocks
of geese passed overhead through a
gray sky. A black squirrel carried
mouthfuls of leaves to a nest being
built near the top of one of the
hemlocks. A deer came into view.
Moving slowly and feebly, the animal
walked close to camp rather than
trying to avoid it. The deer is
being pursued, Rand told himself
when he noticed the blood-covered
arrow stuck in the animal's side. A
chattering, alarm call from a
squirrel also alerted Rand. Without
moving, he watched the deer's back
trail. In a short time, the sound
of a twig snapping came from this
direction. Afterward, Rand saw
something move before the form of a
person became visible among tree
trunks and branches. An Huron
hunter, Rand exclaimed to himself.
He's tracking the deer.

Following the blood-spotted
path left by the deer, the Huron
passed the camp. He reappeared
carrying the deer. This man walked
westward, proceeding around the main
pond. He's returning to his
encampment beside Spring Creek,
reasoned Randin.

When a pink glow, along the
western horizon, vanished to be

replaced by pale light from a veiled moon, Rand left his camping place and started walking around the western side of the large pond. Having passed this stretch of water, he waded into Spring Creek and followed its route through the woods.

A clamor of honking calls spoke from a murky sky and marked the route of a passing flock of geese. Rand stepped cautiously through cold water. Pushing his pack forward for buoyancy, he alternately walked and swam while following a bank topped by aged willows. His movements became awkward when chilling water numbed his muscles. A beaver swam close to the opposite bank then a muskrat crossed the creek's calm surface.

An heron watched the man pushing a pack of supplies downstream. In front of a lean-to, on the north bank, the pack and man stopped moving until ripples on the stream had dissipated. The bundle stirred again. It was pushed to the bank then the man held this bundle when he crawled out of the water. He walked passed the shelter and proceeded northward to high, rocky ground where the outline of a person was etched against a pale sky. The form was also brightened by light from a fire.

Rand stepped closer to the person sitting on the rocks like a natural part of the land's contour. Moving toward the side of the person, Rand saw the woman's face outlined by firelight. Her features were slightly wrinkled although these lines portrayed experience and knowledge with no trace of feebleness. The woman looked at Rand and her expression did not seem to change.

She spoke softly to Rand, using words he didn't understand. "Hello woman," he whispered. "Thanks for not alarming the others."

Relieved that the woman had not yet called out for help, Rand stepped quickly away from her and hurried toward the canoes. Seeing his canoe, he pulled it into the water.

Clouds broke in the overcast sky, bringing an increased sheen of moonlight onto the landscape. A dog barked inside the lean-to. People started talking inside the structure.

A dog left the lean-to, ran along the creek's bank and yapped at

113

Rand.   He paddled quickly and moved out of view beyond gnarled willows bordering the water.

Why didn't the woman call for help?   Randin asked himself while paddling downstream among shadows. There was help for her in the camp. She could have yelled and I would've been outnumbered.   I think, however, she was not a person who can be scared easily.   She could see and sense I was not going to harm her. In return, she spared my life by not calling to the others.   I now have one pack of essential supplies and I have recovered my canoe.   I could return southward to my trading post. Yet winter is coming and I need trapping and trading supplies.   I didn't travel this far to just return with nothing.   I have one, large advantage in my favor and that is the fact they will not be expecting me to return to their camp.   I think I'll at least try to go back and get my supplies.   The dog, though, is a problem.   His barking always alarms the camp. Maybe, if I am talking to the woman again, the dog will accept me and not bark at me.   That would be a risky course to take.   I must get some food for the dog.   Dogs are always hungry. If I throw food near the shelter, the dog would be too busy eating to bother me.

Scattered clouds moved away from the moon, bringing another period of increased brightness to the forest. Using this extra light, Rand paddled to a solid section of the bank. Acting silently as well as swiftly, he stepped out of his craft and hid it among willows. Next he cut a maple sapling and sharpened its point to make a spear.

After wading in the water, Randin stopped and waited until there was, on the creek, an undisturbed film of moonlight. A frog splashed near Rand, sending ripples undulating under the film of moonlight. The stream's surface settled again, mirroring the same clear patterns of light mixed with shadows.

No sounds disturbed the night's solitude. I'm not being followed, Rand thought. They must have gone back to sleep in the shelter. The woman is probably continuing to sit beside her fire. Maybe she is a person who is interested in medicine along with the spirit world. She was likely praying or reflecting upon the spirit life of this swamp when I disturbed her. She was probably pleased to see me leave her to her thoughts and visions.

When a fish's fin broke through the sheen on the creek's surface, Rand thrust his spear forward. It stuck into a powerfully struggling salmon. Rand pushed upward with the spear and a silver swirl of spray followed the form of a fish as it came out of the water and hit the bank.

Rand prepared a fire and spitted the salmon on sticks held above the flames. After the meat had roasted sufficiently, he removed large, juicy chunks and ate ravenously, saving half of this meat for the dog.

Having prepared his pack for traveling, he put it in the canoe. He placed the remaining portion of cooked salmon on the floor beside the pack. Stepping into his craft, he sat down and started paddling silently upstream toward the camp.

Randin thought he heard a sound he could not distinguish. I don't really think I heard something, he told himself. I'm bothered by the lack of sounds. The night is too quiet. Usually I feel at home in the woods; but now I have a cold sensation of impending, or present, trouble. I must be among others who are hunting me.

Rand stopped paddling his canoe. The ripples it had caused gradually dissipated, leaving the creek's surface calm until Rand noticed other ripples moving away from water lilies. In the midst of these lilies, water splashed upward and poured away from the rising form of a man. The man's hand moved backward before shooting forward, sending something whirling through the air and coming directly toward Rand's head. He felt the pain, saw a flashing light then slumped forward in his canoe.

Randin regained consciousness and felt pain pulsing in his head. He saw the flames and above him there was a frame of poles forming a shelter. He lost consciousness again.

He woke up facing flames. He was in a lean-to with other people. Three of the men wore deerskin clothing. Two of these men were large while the third man was shorter and leaner. The short man is the hunter I saw near my camp, Rand recalled. He shot the deer and carried it away. He also seems to be the one who threw something—probably a tomahawk—and hit me on the side of my head. This man is a good woodsman. The younger woman seems to be his wife. She is pretty as well as talkative. The older woman is the person I met beside the fire on the hill. The fourth man, wearing a robe, is French.

"The Englishman is awake," said the robed man. He spoke with only a slight trace of an accent. "How does your head feel?"

"My head aches," replied Randin.

"It should ache," said the same man. "Your head ran into a tomahawk."

"I'm lucky the thing just grazed the side o' my head," said Rand before he sat up, causing an extra bolt of pain to rush through his head. He was resting on boughs in a lean-to. The forest was gray with the first rays of golden light flashing from the rising sun.

"You slept through yesterday," explained the man.

"Am I a prisoner here?" asked Rand while he continued to note the people in the camp. The young, robust woman, who seemed to be giving people a lot of instructions and orders, was preparing food beside a fire with many coals and a little flame. The older woman helped with this work.

"You are a prisoner until we know what you are doing," said the robed man.

"What are you doing here?" asked Rand.

"I am Father Fernier, a Jesuit," he answered. "You would say I am a member of the Society of Jesus." Pointing to the short man who had started to help the women with the cooking, the Jesuit said, "My friend who threw the tomahawk is Sandaqua, or Eagle. He is helping his wife. She is called Tochingo, or Crane. The other men are hunters. They are related to Crane and also to her mother, the woman you met. She is the clan mother, a noted healer and spiritual woman among the Hurons. Her name in English would be Touch the Sky. You are an English trader?"

"Yes," answered Randin. "I'm Randin—or Rand—Blake."

"You are a long way from home," said Father Fernier.

"Yes," said Rand, "and so are you."

"I'm not so far away as you might think," replied Father Fernier. "I am from a mission, north of here, called Sainte-Marie. We are working with the Hurons. Touch the Sky wanted to come here because she says this swamp is a spiritual place. When Touch the Sky wants to do something, we do it. She says you are not to be harmed so you will not be harmed unless you cause some trouble."

"Thank her for me," said Rand.

After Father Fernier spoke to the older woman in a soft sounding language, he said to Rand, "Touch the Sky says you are welcome to stay here."

"Ask her if I can have my packs and canoe?" said Rand.

"She has already told the others you can keep your canoe in addition to the pack you retained with you and half of the others. She says her family can use only half of your packs."

"Thank her again for me," said Rand and Father Fernier spoke to her.

After smiling brightly, she brought to the two men bowls of soup along with pieces of bread. Rand tasted the hot broth then said to Father Fernier, "Good soup."

"It's corn soup," explained the Jesuit who also savored the hot broth. "It's the national food of the Hurons—and so is the corn bread. I like them both."

"Bread is delicious too," exclaimed Randin. "I was hungry and thirsty."

"You are also very lucky," said the Jesuit. "Why were you coming back to this camp? Were you going to attack us?"

"I was returning to get my packs," he explained. "I'm a trader and trapper. I can't do much without my supplies."

"This is French trading territory," stated the Jesuit.

"We are at peace now," countered Rand. "Maybe the Hurons, along with the Ojibway and other Algonkians, would like to trade with the English."

"The French traders don't want their furs going to the English," said Father Fernier.

"Peaceful trade is better than war," replied Rand.

"Yes," said Father Fernier. "The French also want their trading territory to remain for French traders only. You will not be harmed. You can leave when you feel well enough to travel."

"Whom do I thank for my safety?" asked Randin. "Do I thank Touch the Sky?"

"I am a Jesuit," replied the man coolly. "I seek souls, not furs or war. I should say, though, that if Touch the Sky wanted you killed, you would not be alive now. What happened when you met her beside the fire?"

"We did not—could not—speak," said Randin after he had finished the flavorful soup and bread. Touch the Sky removed the empty, pottery bowls then Randin said, "We understood we meant no harm to each other although we didn't say anything. What's in the tasty soup?"

"Corn, beans, squash and venison," answered the Jesuit. "The bread is made from corn."

"My headache isn't as bad now," said Randin. "The food helped. What do you do at Sainte-Marie?"

"We have a church there," answered the Jesuit. "I was sent to the Hurons because I learn languages easily. Touch the Sky comes to my church at Sainte-Marie. She wanted to show me her church. What else could I do? I came here to see her church. The shorter man is her husband. The other men are from her family—her longhouse family. Because this is her special, spiritual place, the men only do enough hunting to get necessary food. There is no extra hunting done here because Touch the Sky says the animals need places where they can rest and renew themselves. Without such places, the animals, along with birds, fish and plants, would die and we would all suffer."

Tochingo served the men coffee in metal cups. "Thank you," said Rand. "I recognize the cups. Should I also recognize the coffee?"

"Oui," said the Jesuit, smiling. "The coffee comes from the packs we are allowed to keep. Touch the Sky is a spiritual leader as well as a Clan Mother. Tochingo is a strong leader and will probably be a Clan Mother some day." After sipping his drink, he added, "The coffee is good."

"Yes, it is," agreed Rand. "Can you also speak the Ojibway language?"

"Yes," answered Father Fernier. "They speak the Algonkian language like the other Algonkian nations. I speak the Iroquoian language of the Hurons. Their language is the same as other Iroquoian nations such as the Neutral, Tobacco, Erie and the Six Nations of the Iroquois Confederacy. The Iroquois Confederacy and the English are at war with us."

"You are at war too?" asked Randin to annoy the man.

"I am French," the Jesuit replied.

"You can't be at war because you are interested only in souls," said Randin.

"I am also French," replied the man coolly. "You are free to leave, however, because Touch the Sky says you must not be harmed."

"Would you have my packs put in my canoe?" asked Rand.

"Oui," he said before speaking in the pleasant sounding language and the two hunters walked to hides covering some packs. Hides were removed and bundles were placed in the canoe. The special pack of supplies was also added to the craft.

Speaking English again, Father Fernier said to Randin, "My political orders are to stop the

Hurons and Algonkians from trading southward with the Iroquois and English."

"Do you agree with your political instructions?" asked Randin.

"No," he answered. "I am a Jesuit. I prefer trade to war."

"Do you think the war will return?" asked Randin.

"Yes," he replied. "The Iroquois and their English traders will push northward and cause a war."

"Why not trade instead of fight?" asked Randin.

"We want the furs to go east to Montreal and Quebec City," stated Father Fernier. "We don't want our fur trade to go south to the English and Iroquois."

"Before I leave," said Randin, "would you translate for me so I can talk to Touch the Sky."

"Yes," he answered, smiling. "She has already told me she wants to talk to you before you go."

"Do you get along well with her?" asked Rand before he stood up. His head throbbed slightly. He stepped forward and got the coffeepot that had belonged to him. Touch the Sky had supervised the loading of the canoe. When she approached the fire, she was carrying an empty cup. Rand filled it for her then refilled the Jesuit's cup. Rand poured steaming coffee into his own cup before he sat down again on the mattress of boughs. Touch the Sky sat next to him. The Jesuit sat on the other side of Rand. They sipped coffee while watching the fire and camp. Tochingo spoke sharply to Sandaqua who started walking along the creek's bank. The two hunters lurked around the camp although they stayed away from the lean-to.

"I thought priests and medicine people competed with each other and didn't get along well," said Rand.

"A Clan Mother is a political leader as well as a spiritual person," replied the Jesuit. "I have to be respectful of her in both cases. We agree about most things."

Touch the Sky spoke to Father Fernier then he translated her words, saying, "We met at night beside the fire. We were just two people and we respected each other. We wished no harm to each other. In such a way, the Creator meets us and expects us to welcome each other. By the way you met me, I recognized you as a person who knows and understands the Creator. Therefore, I did not call for you to be harmed and I have said no injury will be done to you."

Following an interval when only the snapping fire broke the silence, the woman continued speaking and Father Fernier translated, saying, "The Black Robe and I get along well because we talk to each other. After long talks, we discovered we were talking about the same things. We spoke of one Creator who made the earth and all things in it. The Creator can continue to be heard through a spiritual presence in the land. From this spiritual center, all good in life comes. Life lasts forever. The purpose of life is to walk with the Creator, experiencing all there is to experience. If the Creator existed in only one form, there could be no awareness that comes through experiencing differences. We appreciate the warmth of summer after we have been through the cold of winter. We enjoy the presence of the Creator after we have walked farther away. There is a limit to how far we can get from the Creator because life forms are aspects of the Creator.

All things have a purpose in life and can find their purposes when they do the will of the Holder of the Heavens."

"Does a priest have belief's that are different from the views of the medicine people, like Touch the Sky?" Rand asked the Jesuit. "I've been told the priests have different beliefs."

"We don't have a different view," replied the Jesuit. "I have only an additional view. I came not to take away but to add. My mission is to add Christ to the beliefs of all people in order to help them come closer to God rather than be away. The greater distance people are away from God, the more trouble they have. We want to experience life forever with the Creator and not away from the Creator. Belief in Christ brings a person quickly back to God."

"I can see why you were able to agree with each other," said Rand. "Does anyone mind if I go to my special pack to get pipes and tobacco?"

Father Fernier translated Randin's request for Touch the Sky. She spoke to the Jesuit then stood up and stepped to the far side of the lean-to. "She said you won't need your pipes because she has a present for you," explained Father Fernier.

When Touch the Sky sat down again, she held a leather bag. It was brightly patterned with porcupine quills. From this container, she withdrew pipes and tobacco. She gave a pipe to Randin and kept one for herself. Father Fernier removed a similar pipe from his robe. Touch the Sky passed around a pouch of fragrant tobacco. From this pack, tobacco was removed and the pipes were filled. A burning stick from the fire was exchanged to light the tobacco. Before lighting her pipe, Touch the Sky stood up and sprinkled tobacco into the fire. She spoke softly while tobacco smoke mixed with other smoke rising above the flames. Returning to her usual place on the boughs, she lit her pipe then spoke to Father Fernier.

To Randin, Father Fernier explained, "Touch the Sky says you don't have to go to your packs because she has tobacco for us. She has given me the pipe I am using. She made it. She also made her pipe and the one you are using. She has given you the pipe. As you can see, it is a black, pottery pipe with a bird on the bowl facing the smoker."

"Thank her for the present," said Rand.

When the Jesuit spoke to the woman, she smiled brightly at Randin. To Randin, the Jesuit said, "Touch the Sky is a traditional, medicine person and a Christian. The same is true for the rest of us."

After sending a particularly long tendril of smoke out toward the campfire, Randin noted the lurking presence of the other four people in the camp. They seemed to be busy although Rand knew he was always being watched. These are sensible people, he said to himself. They are being careful.

"We offer you your canoe, some of your supplies and a chance to return home," said Father Fernier.

Thinking of going home, Randin realized he felt he was at home in this swamp. He had briefly forgotten he was supposed to be a stranger here, being watched by other people. "What is the most interesting thing you have learned from Touch the Sky?" he asked the Jesuit.

Father Fernier smoked his pipe, sending a whiff of smoke drifting toward the other four people sitting and talking on the bank of the creek. "She said we are all parts of the Creator and we live forever to experience life. Walking away from the Creator causes trouble and moving closer brings happiness. The most interesting thing she said, though, would have to be that we are not only parts of the Creator but we, accordingly, live forever and we can come to earth often as well as go back. We return to earth as people, if we wish, and we can go back in visions."

These thoughts took Rand to a concerning topic. "I can trade here?" he asked.

"In God's hands there is always agreement and justice," answered the Jesuit. "In the hands of the world, there's not always agreement or justice."

"The Iroquois are running short o' beavers," replied Rand. "The trading business is not improving with the English colonies and the Dutch. These traders will be looking to the northwest to get furs, like I did."

"I fear the northern push," replied the Jesuit.

"Why don't you leave?" asked Rand.

"Only in Christ there is hope," he answered. "You are the one who should leave. You are too far ahead o' your time here. You have done your best. Now go home while you can."

"I haven't failed by coming here," said Rand. He enjoyed smoking the pipe and he felt at home in this shelter, talking to Father Fernier and Touch the Sky. The other people were waiting and watching. Sunlight, dropping among trees in the forest, created green and yellow hues that combined to provide a peaceful atmosphere as if the forest was resting. "I came here to trade or trap for furs," continued Randin. "I have received more than furs. I can leave with a feeling of accomplishment."

"Nothing worthwhile is easy to achieve," said Father Fernier. "All good things seem to come to us through difficulty as gold must be heated to get it from the stone."

"I'll return to the southern, trading post," said Rand. "Thank you for your help and information.

Please also thank Touch the Sky for me."

The Jesuit talked to Touch the Sky and she spoke to Rand. Her face brightened and she continued speaking softly. Father Fernier, translating, said, "You have acted bravely to come here. You have done well. We can't always see the results, or accomplishments, of our efforts. We can only strive to do our best and some day, when we walk to the spirit world, we can more clearly look forward as well as back and then we will see where we have been. We are all parts of the Creator. Therefore we can find companionship with the trees, birds, animals and people. The Black Robes have a church at Sainte-Marie. I brought this Black Robe here so he could see the place where I can most comfortably talk to the Creator. Return to your home in the south, Randin Blake, and—if only in my visions—we will meet again. Every person we meet brings us a gift. You have given us information and we also thank you for the trade goods. If you have tried your best, do not think you have failed. Remember we can't always see the results of our work. I come here to meet the spirit in this swamp. The area is also a refuge for trees, birds and animals. I feel at home here and I wish the same experience for all who pass this way."

"In the swamp, I now have a home and I thank you both for showing it to me," said Rand before he stood up. "My head feels better. Thanks for the pipe," he added to Touch the Sky. He slipped the black, pottery pipe into his pocket.

She spoke to Father Fernier. Afterward, he said to Rand, "Touch the Sky hopes you will enjoy the pipe. When you smoke it, she asks you to think about us. Remember too, your home in the swamp. In such a way, your friends and home, including the Creator, will always be with you."

To Touch the Sky and Father Fernier, Randin said, "Thank you." He walked to his loaded canoe, stepped inside and sat down in his comfortable craft. Picking up his paddle, he dipped it into the cool water then pushed forward while turning the blade, steering his canoe into the center of the stream. He looked back and waved to the people who waved to him from the camp.

Randin paddled his canoe along a calm surface mirroring surrounding banks and trees along with a narrow strip of sky. Having a feeling of accomplishment, he thought, I came here to trade for furs and, in return for my trade goods, I received goods of indescribable value. I received a reminder I have company in this forest and in my life.

Daniel Hance Page

FOUR

THE LOGGERS

1850

Edna Carver believed it could never happen to her; but she had proven herself to be wrong because she really was lost. Edna sat down and watched a pale glimmer of moonlight softly touch the frozen forest after the storm. Sharply edged drifts of snow cut through the forest and remained as they had been formed by a white, howling wind. She had tried to reach an east-west tote road leading to the logging camp. She didn't find any features of the landscape that she recognized. Patterns of snowdrifts no longer made any sense to her. Throughout the swamp, the drifts pointed in different directions. Snow patterns had been sculptured by an erratic wind, filled with snow and cold enough to leave a patch of frozen skin on her face just below her left eye. While walking, she placed her hand on this hard patch until it thawed and became soft again. The wind itself had seemed to have become lost and swirled in a white frenzy of flailing snow.

Edna was protected from much of the cold because, over her sweater and shirt, she wore an Hudson Bay coat and she also had a muskrat, fur hat. Leggings provided extra protection for her jeans. Her feet were kept warm in moccasins and she used snowshoes to help her walk across the snow.

A strand of grayish black hair protruded from her hat. There were lines on her face although her black eyes sparkled.

The fact that she didn't know where she was had a much more distressing affect on her than she had previously imagined. She felt disoriented because, in the past, she thought she knew each part of the swamp and felt at home in these familiar surroundings. She fought back a growing surge of panic. I have already made enough mistakes for one night, she concluded. I walked half the night before admitting I was lost. Now I realize that, when I don't know where I'm going, I could be anywhere. We've had loggers get lost almost within sight of our camp. Maybe that's where I am now. The camp could be beside me. I should soon be getting the first meal ready for the men. They might not look for me. They might think I just quit because I'm opposed to cutting down the trees. Although I'm a good cook, I maybe shouldn't be working in a logging camp. I'm cooking for the men who are cutting down my friends, the trees. However, I feel better being here during the logging work rather than being absent. Being somewhere else doesn't help. I'm not sure what good I'm doing by being here. Maybe I can worry the loggers so they won't take too many trees. I always wanted to come to this swamp because of my ancestor, Night Star. They say I'm like her. We are both spiritual people and very independent. I enjoy visiting the stone caches where she stored her food and lived in the valley. I enjoy cooking for people. The woodcutters are good men. They just don't see this swamp as I see it. There's no money in just looking at trees says the foreman Colby Reese. I don't require a lot o' money. It's necessary for some things like paying bills. All I really need is this swamp. This place is my home.

Night Star said the Great Spirit is here.

Edna's thoughts were interrupted when she saw an Arctic owl's shadow flickering across the moonlit snow. "Messenger," whispered Edna to this passing broad-winged bird. "What are you telling me?" To herself, Edna said, I might be making another mistake; but I'll walk, at least for a short distance, in the direction the Thunderbird traveled.

When Edna stepped on the clean snow, her snowshoes caused squeaking and crunching sounds. She came to a dense stand of cedars. After separating snow-laden branches, she entered an area sheltered by a surrounding wall of cedars. This is an ideal place to rest for the remainder of the night, she concluded.

Using dry, cedar wood, she soon had the companionship of a warming fire. Flames cast light against an interlocking wall of branches. She prepared a mat of boughs beside the fire.

Sitting down on the boughs, Edna was warmed by the fire and protected from the wind by the cedars. She watched the sky and wondered if anyone would be looking for her. In the distance, wolves howled. Closer to the cedars, an owl hooted repeatedly.

Following the resonant hooting calls, silence returned until a branch snapped among the cedars. The cracking branch made a sharply piercing sound in the still night. Flames flickered light against branches inside the protective wall. Some of these branches shook, sending snowflakes shimmering across the firelight.

Edna stood up. She had a stricken feeling. Being lost was enough trouble to cope with for one night, she said to herself. I don't need any more trouble. She picked up a piece of wood protruding from the fire and pointed the burning end of this stick toward the place where a branch had cracked. After separating two, interlocking branches, she peered through this opening and saw the massive, snow-dusted form of a moose. The animal seemed to be resting beside the cedars. The moose also came here for shelter, thought Edna. Maybe the moose is trying to escape from wolves.

Upon seeing Edna and the burning stick, the moose walked away, becoming quickly obscured by snow crested branches. Edna returned to her fire and put the stick back into the flames. She added more wood before sitting down again and resting on her mat of boughs.

She slept beside her fire and was awakened by the crunching sounds of something large walking outside the cedars. She added wood to her fire. Holding a large piece of firewood in her hand, she kept the wood's other end in the flames until this end was blazing.

Something large started crashing through the wall of cedars. Branches cracked and snow fell in long, fine tendrils. A grizzly bear's head appeared through an opening in the wall of branches. More branches cracked and snow tumbled as the rest of the bear's massive body moved into the flickering firelight. The animal stood up on its back legs and extended one front paw to claw the air in front of Edna. She felt herself freeze with the chill of sensing her death was close. Her throat dried and heart pounded.

With a stricken feeling, she watched the head and claws that could be upon her swiftly. To delay death, she jabbed the burning wood upward toward the head. The jaws opened, releasing a bellowing growl. Teeth glistened in the firelight. A second growl answered from outside the cedars.

The grizzly turned its head away from the smoke and flame on the menacing stick. The animal moved with surprising agility and pushed through the encircling cedars. Branches swung back into place while, beyond these trees, vicious snarls erupted. Crunching sounds caused by the walking bear gradually diminished leaving only silence to lurk in the forest.

Edna was trying to settle her nerves and pounding heart when branches stirred again, allowing a dark form to move forward. A flash of fear dissipated as Edna recognized the stray wolf that came to the tent cookhouse to get food. "You're a welcome sight," she exclaimed to the wolf. "You drove away the bear."

Edna placed the burning stick in the fire before she ran her hand along the side of the wolf's head.

Jaws clamped onto her arm and held it briefly in the wolf's usual way of greeting. "I don't have much food to share with you right now although you've saved my life," she said to the animal watching her. "My torch and my friend were too much for the bear. The grizzly turned away. Maybe if I follow your tracks, we'll be able to get back to our cookhouse. I call you Cut Ear because of your split ear. You probably got your cut during the last fight that drove you away from the company of other wolves. You helped to get rid o' the bear."

Edna noted the wolf's clear, yellow eyes. "You are pleased to meet a friend and so am I," she said. "We are both relieved to have the bear retreat into the murky night. There's nothing more loyal than a well treated dog or wolf."

Upon relaxing, Edna felt exhaustion sweep through her. Rather than fight fatigue, she let it sweep through her and she slept on the mat of boughs.

Awakening at daybreak, she said to the wolf resting on snow beside the mat, "Cut Ear, let's go home. We'll get some treats. I'm going to

follow you and see if you will lead
me back to the cookhouse."

Edna knew the wolf associated
the sound of the word, home, with
the cookhouse and the word, treat,
meant food. Hearing the words
spoken by Edna, Cut Ear stepped
through the thicket of cedars. Edna
followed. Usually she picked the
route and the wolf checked other
trails and scents while staying with
the path Edna selected. This time,
however, Edna tried to let Cut Ear
lead. The course the wolf took was
winding with a few side diversions,
although the guide seemed to be
heading in one main direction. She
hoped the wolf was returning to the
logging camp.

I haven't been able to get into
a routine of life, Edna reflected as
she followed the wolf tracks in the
snow. I have an husband, children
and many other family members along
with friends. To complicate things,
I am a spiritual person and an
healer. I also like to cook for
people and I'm a cook for the
loggers working in this swamp.
Being a cook at the logging camp
might seem normal to most people.
Such work, however, is a
contradiction to my beliefs because

I'm helping loggers to cut down trees in my swamp. I've tried to explain my actions by realizing the men would do the same work if I wasn't here and someone else did the cooking. I feel better being present rather than being absent. I can do my best when I'm at the camp to present my point of view. I've told them this swamp is a particularly spiritual place. Wildlife must not be harmed in the swamp unless there's a real need for the food. Trees should not be cut unless such cutting is a vital necessity. This area is the home of my ancestor, Night Star. By continuing my work, maybe I'll find something belonging to her. Possibly I can discover some of the knowledge she learned in such a spiritual forest. She said the Great Spirit lives in places like Spirit Swamp. I am now lost in the swamp and following the tracks of a stray wolf. Cut Ear seemed to be alone so I placed food for him behind my tent at the camp. Gradually, he learned to trust me. I'm possibly the one friend he trusts so he followed me in this swamp and helped to drive away the bear. By saying the word, treats, to him, I hope I have reminded him of the food in my cook tent and he is leading me to my tent. He knows where the camp is located. He should also associate the word, home, with my tent.

Looking ahead, among the trees, Edna saw the wolf. He was standing and waiting for her to catch up to him. Upon seeing her, he turned swiftly and ran ahead, vanishing out of view beyond a spray of snow.

I still don't know where I am, she said to herself. I hope Cut Ear is leading me back to my comfortable cook tent. I feel at home here in my swamp; however, I'm getting tired. I would like to rest and prepare food along with coffee.

Because of increasing fatigue, Edna stopped appreciating the rhythmical whisper of her snowshoes rustling across the snow. She no longer noticed the lines and patterns of drifted snow glistening in patches of sunlight slanting between towering trees. Increasingly, she started to feel a gnawing sense of worry. I am lost, she reminded herself. I don't like the way my nerves are tightening. I don't think I should be walking so far when I don't know where I'm going. I'm in a strange situation. A wolf is guiding me. I trust Cut Ear, but does he know I want him to go to my cook tent? Maybe the wolf is taking me to the part of this swamp where he lives.

The route Edna followed became gradually rougher until she realized she had entered a particularly wild section of the swamp. Flat surfaces indicated an endless series of snow and ice covered ponds. Tangles of branches and gnarled trunks of willows cast an eerie spell across the swamp. There was also a gripping silence to this seemingly ageless place. A fitful breeze occasionally dislodged snow from branches, sending shimmering tendrils dropping through shafts of sunlight.

I wonder if I should be entering this timeless realm, Edna said to herself. Maybe this land is intended for the wolf and I should not be here. Yet the wolf has invited me. He's probably taking me to his home rather than to my cook tent. The region resembles a place that no person has entered previously.

She came to a game trail where Cut Ear's tracks were more difficult to follow. She had to stop occasionally to wait for Cut Ear to come back and check on her progress. During her journey into the remote section, she noted the prints of a deer, moose, lynx, cougar and wolverine. There were smaller as well as more numerous, tracks of rabbits, squirrels and porcupines.

Edna was stirred by the wild solitude of the swamp with its ice and snow covered ponds. Aged willows were numerous. Their gnarled shapes contrasted sharply with the straighter trunks of poplars, maples and hickories. In the distance, massive oaks and stately white pines were etched against clouds moving slowly in a scarlet sunset. In an indirect way, the wolf tracks were leading to an hill.

An Arctic owl watched the snowy world from the top of a pine stump on the hill. Beyond the owl, along the crest of the hill, a breeze stirred pine boughs. Behind the upturned roots of a fallen maple, below the stump, the wolf sat down and waited, watching his back trail. Edna continued following Cut Ear's tracks until she saw him and approached him.

The upturned roots provided an hollow containing snow marked by Cut Ear's prints. Trails extended in all directions. "So this is your idea of home," said Edna to the watching wolf. "When I said home, I meant my home, not yours," she added, smiling at the thought of a wolf sharing his home with her. "Now that we've established where home is, let's go and get some treats."

Cut Ear left his resting-place and started walking along the same trail he had just used to reach the hollow. Edna followed him. I hope, this time, Cut Ear knows where he's going, she said to herself. Even though I'm hungry as well as tired and night is upon us again, I have enjoyed seeing Cut Ear's territory. There are no signs that people have ever been here. I feel at home in this place. I am aware of what Night Star reported about the swamp. In such places a person is more aware of being in the presence of the Great Spirit. I can sense myself being, along with all things, part of the Great Spirit. I was fortunate to come to this region. Since the journey has made my body weak and tired, my spirit has become more prominent and I know the Great Spirit walks with me.

She stopped and watched the beauty of the forest, having a new, spiritual perspective. I see now the spirit world, she reflected, and I have come home.

Edna rested beside the trunk of a fallen willow. She started a fire then prepared a mattress of boughs. She gave in to fatigue and slept on the boughs. While she was sleeping, Cut Ear returned and slept beside the camp. During the night, freezing rain pelted the forest, coating trees and snow with ice.

The rising sun shone on the iced landscape, tinting it with a golden sheen. This light illuminated the swamp. Edna saw a grizzly walking in the distance. Grizzlies are small today compared to the great, legendary bears painted on walls in the caves, noted Enda. Maybe hunger occasionally brings the bears out of their winter's hibernation. I hope the word, treats, will now take Cut Ear to my camp. The word, home, took him back to his section of this swamp. Such a walk into one of the wildest areas of the swamp brought me closer to the spirit of the land.

Edna's snowshoes broke through a thin crust of surface ice before sinking into the snow. When the snowshoes came up again, they sent pieces of ice rattling across a sunlit layer of ice. Trees creaked when a breeze moved branches. The forest glistened and shimmered under a clear sky.

Edna followed Cut Ear passed the clump of cedars where she had camped. The wolf proceeded onward, maintaining one main course with a lessening number of diversions. During one of these turns, he rushed at several large, darting forms. He grabbed one of the forms amid a cloud of feathers. Edna hastened to the site and was pleased when the wolf let her take the turkey.

She quickly started a fire and spitted the bird over the flames. After steam shot through holes cut in the golden colored, and crispy skin, Edna removed large, steaming chunks of roasted meat. She shared the pieces with Cut Ear and they both enjoyed a fine meal. "I didn't realize how hungry I was," she said to the wolf. "You have saved my life again. When you first visited me at the cook tent and I fed you, I possibly saved your life. You have now saved me twice and are likely leading me to my camp. Since we are all parts of the one Creator, there are no coincidences. All things are connected through the spirit. When I saved you, I didn't realize I was helping myself."

Traveling again, the wolf walked first and, as usual, stopped and waited occasionally until Edna caught up to him. When Cut Ear was waiting in a clearing, Edna could not initially believe he was standing on a tote road. A warm feeling flashed through her as she recognized the familiar opening in the woods.

Strangely, the wolf didn't rush ahead again. He waited, standing on the road, and seemed to be checking a scent or listening to something.

After approaching Cut Ear, Edna rested and listened until she could hear faint sounds, resembling the crunching noises of horses' hooves tapping against the icy road. In a short time, a team of horses came into view. They were pulling a sleigh containing the camp foreman, Colby Reese. He was a large man who looked even bulkier in his sheepskin coat. A blue woolen hat slanted across the top of his head. He had a wide, frost edged moustache in addition to thick eyebrows and black eyes.

After stopping the horses beside Edna, he said, "I had to know for sure. I've been lookin' for you since the storm."

"I got turned around in the snow," exclaimed Edna. "Cut Ear found me, helped drive off a bear and showed me the way back to camp. From now on, I'm really going to look after that wolf."

"We've all missed you," said Colby. "The food has been terrible. Worst of all has been the coffee. With a good cup o' coffee and a cigar, I can tolerate almost anything."

Enda stepped up onto the sleigh. Colby turned the horses and they were eager to get back to camp. Cut Ear ran behind the sleigh during the journey along the tote road.

"I was very close to camp when I got lost," explained Edna.

"That's usually the way," answered Colby. "When Cut Ear came to the door of the cook tent, I told him to go and get Edna. He looked at me for a moment then left our camp. Likely he knows your name and did go to get you. We often underestimate a wolf, or dog, and all animals or birds. They size up people quickly. Critters know their friends."

"When you have a dog, or wolf, for a friend, you always have a friend," replied Edna. "There's going to be a special spot in the cook's tent for Cut Ear."

"We are all goin' to be pleased to have our cook with us again," stated Colby.

The horses didn't have to be directed to return to camp. The air was cold. A light breeze loosened ice and snow from trees. The sleigh passed a pile of logs beside the road.

"I'd like you to not cut trees any farther into the swamp," said Edna. "I don't want anyone cutting down the swamp."

"You don't have to worry as I told you before," replied Colby. "I don't know how safe the ice is on the ponds and there are very few pines in the low, wet areas. I'm not interested in willows. Around the swamp, there are a lot of trees. As I have said before, there's no money in just lookin' at trees."

"Money is the lowest value of a tree or a forest," said Edna. "I can see taking a few trees or a good number of trees. No one should cut down the whole forest. I take water from the spring for coffee. No one should take all the water."

"Is that your secret for making good coffee?" asked Colby. "You take water from the spring?"

"Yes," she answered.

"I respect trees," added Colby. "I have to cut them. I'm a logging camp foreman."

"One can cut a few trees; but one must never destroy the forest," said Edna.

"You're more definite with your views now than you were before you got lost," observed Colby.

"I got lost in the woods," said Edna. "This experience gave me a chance to find myself and clarify my essential beliefs. The forest is my home. There is a spirit in this swamp."

"I know you believe in spirits," commented Colby.

"I don't believe in spirits," said Edna. "There is only the Great Spirit who created all the world and all things including this swamp."

When the sleigh approached the camp, a man on top of a pile of logs shouted and waved at Edna and the foreman. "The men will be happy to see you," said Colby. "I have missed talking to you."

Tents of the logging camp loomed into view. The sleigh stopped beside the cook tent. "See you for supper," said Colby after Edna stepped off the sleigh.

"Thanks for looking for me," she replied. The sleigh moved away, leaving Edna and Cut Ear standing on the path leading to the cook tent. Cut Ear walked toward this tent. He waited beside a wooden door hinged between two trees at the front of a large tent. Edna opened the door and followed Cut Ear inside the familiar shelter. A wood stove was located centrally at the far end beyond tables and chairs. Cut Ear stretched out on a rug beside the stove while Edna added paper, kindling and wood to the stove then struck a match, bringing its flame to the paper. Flames swarmed over paper and wood before starting to make the regular, thumping sounds of a steadily burning fire. The tent warmed quickly.

Picking up a bucket and pot, she started walking toward the door. Cut Ear moved swiftly and, after the door had been opened, he left the tent ahead of Edna. They walked northwest toward the spring.

Raucous calls of crows rang across the landscape. Four crows flew erratically around a lofty, white pine beside the path leading to the spring.

Edna looked up at the top of the pine. Stirred gently by a breeze, rugged boughs were etched sharply against a cloud-strewn sky. An Arctic owl was clearly outlined against a background of dark boughs. Watching the bird, Edna also noticed the beauty of the tall trunk descending to drifts curving beside the path. In this trunk, there were two large holes. The holes would be joined inside the tree, making an hibernation cavity for raccoons, Edna reasoned. According to tracks in the snow, the raccoons live in this tree and visit my cook tent. Pieces of wood scattered at the base of the trunk show that the coons have been scratching out a larger living space.

Peering into the lowest opening in the trunk, she picked up pieces of loose wood and dropped them on the snow. The raccoons have a fine home here, she thought. I'll place food in this hollow for my friends.

Edna proceeded to the spring and filled the containers with pure water. Upon returning to camp, she prepared a meal of stew for herself, the men and Cut Ear.

During the following days, she had a feeling of being more at home in the swamp than she had been previously. When she was lost, she learned more about herself along with Cut Ear and the forest.

To have time to consider all the things that had been happening to her, she walked with Cut Ear to her place of solitude beside a small section of the pond formed by the spring. She replaced the mattress of boughs on the ledge of ground. This ground sloped to the pond covered by ice and snow.

In front of the mattress of boughs, Edna built a large fire and roasted a turkey over the flames. While the meat cooked, she used an axe to chop ice away from the edge of the pond. She removed a section of ice then waited for the shallow water to clear before obtaining water to prepare wild rice tea.

She was filling the pot when she noticed the smooth, round form in mud at the bottom of the pond. Placing her hand into the chilling water, she stuck her fingers into the soft earth and removed a round objet. Recognizing it as being a bowl, she rubbed it with her hands and rinsed it until she trembled with the cold and excitement. This is a beautiful, pottery bowl, she exclaimed to herself. It contains a stone amulet of a thunderbird. The amulet is much like the one I carry with me.

Edna reached into her pocket and removed a leather pouch. Her fingers trembled as they grasped and uncovered the stone carving. Holding the two amulets, she realized she was staring at two thunderbirds and, according to their shapes along with other markings, the same person had made the two carvings. My ancestor, Night Star, made my pendant, reflected Edna. She has formed both of these carvings. I have found Night Star's camping place. This is also my special site where I come for solitude. This place must've meant the same to her. I'll return her gifts to the Great Spirit just as I found them.

Edna replaced the bowl and thunderbird. She returned her amulet to its leather pouch then walked to the pine and placed the pouch inside the hollow. I'll put my gift here and it can join with the present from Night Star. I have come home.

Looking up at the top branches of the pine, Edna could not see the owl. The forest was silent except for a soft, whirring of a breeze moving among pine boughs. I'll have to tell Colby to spare this tree, Edna said to herself. Each tree is important in the memory of my people and the thoughts of the Great Spirit.

Daniel Hance Page

FIVE

THE TRAPPER

1966

Ceasil Moore thought he had retired from trapping until he, accompanied by his dog, entered the swamp. The dog was called Hound because he was always hunting. Ceas was a lean man of average height. Since the time he had been a barber he used a straight razor to keep his beard neatly trimmed. His years as a carpenter had placed lines in his face. His brown eyes acquired an added sparkle during his walk into the swamp.

Hound was a strong dog with brown and white fur. He was friendly and loyal only to Ceasil. Apparently, according to Hound, other people were not entirely to be trusted and anything else could be hunted.

Upon entering the swamp, Ceas realized he had located a natural place for a trap line. He didn't have any carpentry work to do during the winter and a trap line in a section of wilderness close to town would keep him busy.

The snow was marked by tracks of almost all animals and birds that could be expected to be in the region. Ceas identified prints of deer, weasels, porcupines, rabbits, squirrels, beavers, raccoons, muskrats, foxes, coyotes and timber wolves. He was surprised to see the tracks of a grizzly bear. Birds he was able to identify, by prints or sightings, were turkeys, blue jays, ruffed grouse, owls, crows, cardinals, finches and woodpeckers. Ceas decided to concentrate on trapping muskrats and beavers. He would also try to catch some foxes, coyotes and timber wolves.

He discovered a settler's cabin built in the swamp on high ground amid a cleared area overgrown with raspberry bushes and apple trees. He found this cabin when he had been following coyote tracks. They led to a wide patch of trampled and bloodied snow where only a deer's head remained. Hound sniffed around the area while Ceasil placed the deer's head in the forked trunk of an apple tree. The head was positioned to be above the snow yet reachable by the wolves if they were hungry.

In the high, flat region, Ceas found the cabin. It had collapsed under the weight of a winter's snow and ice. The hand-hewn boards were in usable condition as was the stove. I'll live in a tent while I rebuild the cabin, Ceas decided.

Always accompanied by Hound, Ceasil rented a snow machine with a sleigh to help haul all his building, camping, trapping and cooking supplies. After returning the snow machine and buying additional food, Ceas looked forward to living in the swamp. He would build a cabin and do some trapping.

Ceasil Moore put up a tent. Inside this shelter, he constructed a comfortable mattress of boughs. A small, wood stove supplied heat. This stove was also useful for cooking food although he also used a spit over an outside fireplace for much cooking. To get water, he chopped an hole through the ice on an adjacent pond. When he wanted particularly pure water, he walked to the spring at the western end of the connecting ponds. He chopped an hole through thin ice at the edge of the spring and obtained clear water for making tea or coffee.

He shot a ruffed grouse and roasted it on the spit above the outdoor fire. Life is good here, he thought after he had shared the roasted meat with Hound. Ceas sat down on a chair next to his outside fire. He sipped his favorite, green tea and watched the swamp. Gnarled, willow trunks were mixed with some maples, hemlocks and cedars in the surrounding woods. Sections of flat, snow surfaces marked the courses of numerous ponds. Many of them were connected. Most water drained from the spring and flowed through Spring Creek to Willow River. Willow River flowed from the Pine River to Reed Lake.

This swamp is a fascinating and beautiful place, mused Ceas before he drank the last of the tea in his cup. He put his cup on the table in his outside kitchen and reached into his pocket to remove a pipe along with matches and packet of tobacco. Sitting down again, he filled the pipe's bowl with aromatic tobacco then lit it, sending a tendril of smoke drifting upward toward a starlit sky. Hound enjoys the swamp, observed Ceas. The mutt's away much of the day or night. He has many trails and scents to check.

In the morning, I'll start building my cabin. I enjoy using a tent although I'd like to have a more solid shelter built before the blizzards start whistling through the woods.

An owl hooted repeatedly. Wolves seemed to answer by howling from the hilly country to the northwest. Ceas entered his tent, got into his eider down, sleeping bag on the mattress of boughs. Hound stretched out on part of the mattress and they were soon both sleeping.

The dawn was gray and cold. Ceas decided to keep warm by working at his new cabin. He wanted to use the settler's stone basement and cistern. Therefore, the wood on top of the foundation had to be removed. The good boards and beams would be reused in the new cabin. Remnant wood was added to the pile of firewood.

Having removed the old wood from the stonework, Ceas put in place new beams. Next, he constructed the floor. To the flooring, he attached the walls and roof. The new cabin was fashioned rather quickly because he wanted to start trapping.

Ceas worked any time he had sufficient energy during the days or nights. His efforts were completed in a moonlit night. An owl hooted when he folded his tent and stored it in his new building.

The cabin's door, with a window on each side, faced north because this was a particularly wild and interesting region having most of the ice and snow covered ponds. Windows were also located on the other three walls. A bed, or cot, was placed next to the south wall. A chair faced the northern windows. The wood stove was in the center of the room and a kitchenette, consisting mainly of a sink and shelves, stretched along the west wall. Hound slept on a rug covering the floor at the base of the east wall. A path led eastward to an outhouse, built of logs.

With the cabin completed and a warming fire blazing in the stove, Ceas sat on his chair and looked northward through the two windows providing a view of the swamp where shadows patterned flat, snow and ice covered surfaces of the ponds. Hound rested on his rug.

Ceas refilled the dog's water bucket then placed extra food in the other dish.   After pouring green tea into a pottery cup, Ceas returned to his chair.

The slightly flavored, green drink stirred his thoughts. Tomorrow, he said to himself, I'll go hunting and get some meat stored for the harsher days.   Deer stay in this swamp for the winter.   In case they decide to move, I want to have a good supply of meat cached.   I'll have to check the cellar then I can get to my real work of trapping. There are lots o' beaver along these connecting streams and ponds.   I can also get muskrat pelts along with a few foxes and coyotes.   Timber wolves have trails coming from the hills to the north.   I've seen a few lynx tracks.   I'll set snares for rabbits.   I can cook the rabbits on spits or make stew.

After preparing more tea, Ceas sat down again and enjoyed the drink.   I like carpentry work, he reflected.   I have made a comfortable place for Hound and I to live in this swamp.   My real work is trapping.   First I'll shoot some deer, store the meat then set my traps as well as snares.

Ceas finished drinking the tea, put out the oil lamp and went to sleep on his cot. He woke up occasionally and added wood to his stove. A small fire thumped in the stove and warmed the cabin.

In the morning, falling snowflakes whispered through the swamp. Ceas got his rifle along with his toboggan and started to follow one of his old snowshoe paths crossing a flat surface of an ice and snow covered pond. Deer trails crisscrossed the snow. In a trampled area, amid willows, he heard snorting sounds. Turning, he saw a buck standing amid a background of pussy willows. Moving his gun to his shoulder, Ceas aimed quickly and fired. The buck jumped forward and ran out of view beyond tangles of willows.

Hound dashed ahead of Ceas. They both followed a bloodied trail. It led to a dark form of the deer crumpled on the snow.

Ceas butchered the animal, leaving unused parts on the snow while saving most of the meat in addition to the hide. "Animals will be attracted by the remnants we don't use," Ceas said to Hound. "Later we'll trap the foxes and wolves that eat this food. We'll take our meat to the cabin and come back for more."

Ceasil kept hunting until he had enough meat stored to last throughout the winter. I can hunt for fresh meat anytime, he thought. At least I know Hound and I have food. We will now concentrate on trapping. I'll check the basement to make sure my meat will be safe. I have a couple o' places to fix to insure that the walls are secure.

At dawn, following a breakfast of pancakes and coffee, Ceasil started the task of refurbishing the stone foundation. He first checked his supply of meat and was relieved to find it remained frozen in the shallow area of the basement. Lastly, he checked the deeper part and had to replace some fallen sections.

In replacing fallen stones, Ceas discovered that a wall had collapsed because an attached compartment had loosened. In this smaller chamber, he uncovered boxes containing ink, pens and paper. There was also a wooden box sealed with wax.

Ceas took the waxed box up the few steps to the trap door and entered his cabin. He replaced the trap door and prepared tea. He was tired, yet, because of excitement concerning the sealed box, he could not sleep.

The oil lamp provided pleasant, golden light. A fire thumped in the stove. Hound slept beside Ceasil's chair. Ceasil filled his cup with green colored, steaming tea. He put tobacco in his pipe. When it was ready to light, he placed it next to the tea on the new, hand-hewn table. Outside the cabin, wind rustled against frosted windows. A wolf howled from the northern hills.

With all preparations being ready for a pleasant, winter evening inside his cabin, Ceas reached down and picked up the special box. It had been skillfully constructed and fitted together along with being sealed with wax. Ceas partially inserted a knife's blade into the layer of wax between the upper and lower portions of the container. He inserted while twisting the blade and forced the sections to separate with a popping sound. A fine fragrance of cedar escaped from the chamber containing a neat stack of papers tied together with a piece of leather cord. Ceas removed the bundle and placed the two empty sections of the box on the floor next to the sleeping dog.

Ceas held the pine-scented papers. He sipped tea to prolong the excitement and enjoyment of the story the papers might contain. The top sheet contained the title, JOURNAL, 1901.

Daniel Hance Page

SIX

THE JOURNAL

1901

I decided to write a journal and seal the papers in a box because I can't live much longer in my present condition. I know I'm getting weaker. I'm too weak for my legs to mend. A bear broke both my legs. I just can't get around well enough to get food or firewood and do the other work necessary to stay alive. I'm going to do my best to survive. If my best efforts fail, I, at least, want to leave my story in these papers.

I'm a farmer. We have always been farmers. After my wife left, I decided to start a farm in a quiet place. I sold my farm and purchased this swamp. I moved here last spring. The soil is rich. I grew corn along with beans and squash as the Hurons had established these crops in this area many years ago.

Because of insufficient sunlight, the squash plants didn't mature. Squirrels and raccoons ate my corn. Fortunately, the beans grew abundantly. I also planted raspberries and apple trees. I won't be here to harvest the apples or berries. I have used bulrush roots for vegetables to add some variety to a diet of beans.

I caught a lot of fish by making a weir. I froze a large amount of meat and also dried some of it. I did well until bears started raiding my meat racks. Black bears were a nuisance. However, a grizzly arrived and started causing a lot of trouble.

Maybe my troubles all began when I started hunting and trapping in this swamp. I had money to purchase food from town. I thought I would shoot my own food rather than buy it and I think this decision led to all my problems.

I was able to buy this swamp cheaply because the land is so wet. Also there were Indian legends saying this land was a spiritual place. It was also a wilderness refuge, and people must not harm this swamp.

Indian legends didn't worry me. There was much game present. No one had farmed here since the time of the Hurons and the Hurons did not actually do any farming in the swamp. Loggers had cut trees in the surrounding area although trees were not cut in the wet part. The tall trees shaded and thereby ruined my crops except for the beans.

I had enough money to buy food. If I had used money to purchase food rather than start hunting, I think I could have enjoyed an happy life at my cabin.

I liked all the swamp and its critters. Leopard frogs can be heard at night along with whippoorwills. I enjoy the hooting of owls. Geese nest here. Their resonant, honking calls are exciting sounds. Lots of ducks nest in this swamp. A fox comes to my cabin to get food. I also feed wolves. I get sturgeon, whitefish and even a few salmon from my weir.

When I started hunting, problems arrived. I shot ruffed grouse and many deer. My fish and venison drying and smoking racks attracted black bears. Later the grizzly arrived and drove out the black bears.

The grizzly tore apart my drying racks and ate much of the meat. I had food stored in my cellar. When the grizzly was digging into my cellar, I shot this massive creature. The shot didn't seem to harm the bear because it sprang at me. Before I could escape, a paw hit me, breaking my legs. I managed to crawl into my cabin and closed the door. The bear is eating the remainder of the food I was smoking and drying.

I have tied splints to my legs. I don't think they're healing well. I'm having trouble getting around. The bear is always close to my cabin. I'm going to write my journal and put it away before I get too feeble for such work, or any work.

I've had a good life in the swamp. I'm sure I could've stayed longer if I had not put out all the food and attracted a grizzly. This swamp has been my home. The Indian legends say the swamp is a place of refuge for the wilderness. If I had the choice again, I would heed the legends and not do any unnecessary harm to the swamp. I could have purchased food from town. I shouldn't have started hunting because, according to the legends, the area is a refuge. I've enjoyed the time I've had in this place. I should not have started hunting because I didn't really need the food. I am writing my journal because I want to continue the message I've learned and tell others that this swamp is a world of the spirit. All can come here to rest and renew themselves. Such a place is not just for hunters. All creatures are connected and they are protected in the swamp.

Jasper Ridge

Daniel Hance Page

SEVEN

THE WOLVES

Ceasil Moore finished reading the letters. Upon returning these papers to the box, he resealed the container then lit his pipe. So I've heard from the previous occupant of this place, reflected Ceas. Jasper Ridge was killed by a grizzly. There can't be many grizzlies around here now, noted Ceas. I don't have to worry about grizzlies or legends. I've been a barber and a carpenter. Primarily, I'm a trapper. The legends won't mind if I do a little trapping because there are numerous beavers, muskrats and wolves along with other animals in this swamp. Tomorrow morning, I'll start setting my trap line. Maybe I'll start with the timber wolves on the hill because they'll be killing the fur bearing animals such as beavers and muskrats.

Ceasil went to sleep and woke up in a cold cabin. He restarted a fire in the stove and heat quickly returned to the building. He prepared the usual breakfast of pancakes for himself and Hound.

181

Hound drank water while Ceas sipped coffee and checked his traps.

Good to be back to work again, he thought after stepping outside and closing the cabin door. Next he put on his snowshoes. He picked up the rope to his toboggan with one hand. His other hand held his rifle. He started traveling northward, enjoying the familiar feeling of walking on snowshoes.

He proceeded at a steady pace with the snowshoes rhythmically rustling across the snow and ice covered ponds. He crossed Spring Creek then the country road that had been a tote road. He entered another area where flat, snow surfaces indicated the presence of ice covered ponds beneath the snow. Willows were numerous along with maples. Deer trails were accompanied by wolf prints. Wolf tracks became more plentiful until they formed separate paths crisscrossing the hill region.

Beside some wolf trails, the snow had been trampled and contained strands of gray fur. Ceas set traps in such well-used sections.

By holding Hound while pushing a stick into a set trap so the steel jaws exploded upward and clamped onto the wood, Ceas had trained the dog to both remember and fear the scent of all traps. I should get Hound out o' here before he forgets something, Ceas told himself after setting the last trap. Our work is finished. We should get back to our cabin. I don't want to spook the wolves.

Ceasil and Hound returned to their cabin. When night approached, casting a network of shadows across the snow, the moon sparkled during its ascent. Turkeys resting on an oak's branches became silhouetted against a backdrop of the rising moon. Ceas easily shot one then another of these birds before the others flew out of the tree.

He collected the birds and saved one for later use. He spitted the other over a fire. Both man and dog enjoyed slabs of the steaming, roasted, juicy meat.

Having waited restlessly for a few nights, Ceas left the cabin during a cold, gray dawn. Snow squeaked under his snowshoes when he walked over the snow and ice topped ponds. Again he stepped carefully across the flat, snow and ice surface covering Spring Creek. Beyond the road, he followed his old, snowshoe trail leading to the hills.

Upon approaching the slopes, he noticed a form moving above a dark object on the snow. He continued walking and watched until he was certain he could see a tall, timber wolf standing beside another wolf sprawled in the snow.

Ceas waited and continued observing the hillside. Finally, as he suspected, he identified the forms of three other wolves among the willows. He aimed his rifle at the wolf standing beside the sprawled form. The gunshot blasted and echoed through the woods and the second wolf crumpled into a motionless form.

Hound sprang forward. He reached the fallen wolves and a sharp, short snarl revealed to Cease that the wolf with its leg in a trap had been alive. Hound quickly killed the wounded animal.

Reaching the kill site, Ceas noticed fresh blood trickling from both dead wolves. The standing animal had been killed instantly by the gunshot.

Ceas worked quickly to take the hides. He carried them back to his cabin. He hung the two pelts on the outside of the west wall.

During the night, after an owl hooted repeatedly, Ceasil heated some previously cooked, venison stew, preparing a flavorful meal for himself and Hound. Ceas also steeped green tea. He sat on his chair, sipped the tea then filled his pipe. He lit the tobacco, sending a bluish-white tendril of smoke curling toward the ceiling.

There were five wolves and now there are three, he observed. The remaining wolves will be even more difficult to kill because they will have renewed fear of people and dogs in addition to traps and guns. If I don't catch the other wolves quickly, I'll have to leave them and start concentrating on the rest of my trap line. I have to start catching muskrats and beavers.

Ceasil was feeling contented. He had a good supply of food prepared for the coldest part of winter. He had also collected his first two hides. His cabin was comfortable. The oil lamp cast golden light across the board and log walls. There is joy in accomplishment, he reflected before tapping ashes from his pipe and refilling his cup with tea. I've made a fine cabin in this wild swamp. The place looks as wild today as in the earliest times. The gnarled willows are majestically beautiful. Ice covered ponds and streams provide unobstructed surfaces for traveling. Signs of birds and animals are everywhere....

Ceasil was interrupted from his thoughts when Hound stood up and growled. The growl was deep and menacing. Fur bristled along the dog's neck as well as back. Ceas sensed hair standing up on the back of his own neck. A chill coursed through him, making him shiver.

Hound barked loudly as if to make enough noise to drive away an enemy. Startled by the barking, Ceas jumped. His hand flipped upward, shooting tea into his face. The shock of the tea along with continued barking sent him scrambling for his gun.

Holding his rifle and having it ready for firing, Ceas opened the door so Hound would be able to step outside and investigate the threat or drive off the intruder. Ceas felt an icy grip of fear clamp onto his stomach when the dog sniffed the air and wouldn't go outside. Never before had this dog hesitated from investigating something or attacking, Seth told himself.

Light from the oil lamp lit a small section of snow in front of the doorway. Beyond this bright swath, additional light glimmered along trunks and branches in front of a backdrop of pale snow and murkiness. "What is out there?" Ceas asked the tense dog. "Bears should be hibernating. If a bear stirred out of hibernation and was walking around, I'd hear crunching sounds. Something has scared you for the first time in your life. I guess we all have times to be scared." I feel a real pulse of fear myself, Ceas noted. I'm also curious. Maybe I'm being foolish, but I won't be able to sleep unless I know what has bothered Hound.

Stepping back into the cabin and closing the door, Ceas got his flashlight. Opening the door again, he shone a beam of light into the swamp. This beam flickered across tree trunks, branches and snow.

When he walked outside, his boots seemed to crunch too loudly on the snow. Cold out here, he thought, or am I just feeling my own fear. Hound followed me out of the cabin. He must have stayed near the door.

Using the flashlight in one hand while holding his rifle ready to fire in his other hand, Ceas walked around to the eastern side of the cabin. He noted only the usual snowshoe tracks along with boot prints and dog tracks. Moving to the back of the building, he saw more of the same, normal marks.

He walked to the west side of the building, where the hides hung, and his heart pounded faster when he saw the large, fresh, wolf prints under the pelts. Continuing to stare at the fresh tracks, he said to himself, one wolf has followed us to our cabin. We killed two of this animal's family members and now it has tracked us to our home. Our scents would be mixed with the scents of the dead wolves. I know wolves don't bother, and actually fear, people. However, this wolf has come to see what happened to family members of the pack.

An explosion of snarling erupted from the front of the building. Ceas ran toward sounds of vicious, guttural rage and saw Hound tied in battle with a large, black wolf. A piercing, blood-curdling cry issued from Hound before he was shaken like a blanket. Ceas aimed his rifle toward the battle. The wolf dropped the limp form of the dog and sprang away from the rifle's blast. The black animal kept bounding into the murky woods. Ceas probed the darkness with two more shots. Their echoes diminished until only a cold silence stalked the snow.

After pulling Hound into the cabin and closing the door, he checked his friend and found no sign of life. Wolves don't bother people, Ceas reminded himself. Although I have no reason to worry about the wolves, I know I wouldn't be able to enjoy staying in this place any longer. The wolf was after Hound.

Regardless of the fact that wolves don't bother people, this clash has ended my enjoyment of my cabin. I'll pack my equipment. At first light, I'll put my packs and Hound on the toboggan then I'll leave this forest. My trapping career is over. I'll return to my other types of employment. I should've listened to the legends and have realized I was making a

mistake by trying to trap in the
Spirit Swamp.

EIGHT

THE EXCAVATION

Ronald Shellton purchased the area of land known as Spirit Swamp. He bought this land at a reasonable price because legends describing the swamp discouraged other buyers. He liked the idea of having a legend that worried people. Such a legend would work like a fence and provide privacy for a man who liked a quiet life. Shell was a reasonably successful artist and he couldn't think of a better place to paint than a swamp with a legendary fence to keep out intruders.

For a shelter, Ron used a tent heated by a wood stove. He decided to live in tent and his wider home would be Spirit Swamp.

Ron was in an art store buying supplies for his work in the swamp when he saw a woman entering the store. If she is an artist, she is a painter of the wilderness, Ron thought while he noted her outdoor appearance. Her blond hair was tied at the back and swept neatly away from an attractive face with pale blue eyes. She wore a sheepskin-lined, denim jacket over a red shirt. The bottom legs of her jeans were tucked into rubber boots. A traveling pack was strapped to her back and she was looking at wildlife prints.

The woman recognized Ron because he resembled pictures she had seen of him. The man had black, yet graying, hair and brown eyes. He was lean and his clothing resembled those of a woodsman, having a brown jacket over a leather vest and blue, corduroy shirt. He also wore jeans and rubber boots. He was checking supplies by himself and was selecting oil paints.

Upon approaching the man, she asked, "Are you Ronald Shellton?"

"Yes, I think so," he answered.

"Are you sure?" she asked.

"Yes," he answered. "Who are you?"

"Tiana Benton," she replied. "I'm an archaeologist. I wanted to ask you some questions."

"About archaeology?" he asked, intrigued by this attractive woman.

"Yes," she said. There was nothing threatening about this man although he appeared to be strong. She felt he would allow her to investigate the legend of Spirit Swamp. "Do you own Spirit Swamp?"

"Yes," he answered. "I have an apartment in town and I paint in the swamp where I live in a tent."

"A tent?" she asked.

"Yes," he said. "It's a very comfortable home."

"Can I treat you to supper at the restaurant across the street?" she asked. "I have some things to check with you."

"Okay," he replied. He took his paint tubes to the cashier and paid for them. The clerk put them in a bag along with a receipt and Ron left the store. He walked with the blond woman to a restaurant called the Fisherman's Cookery.

The building's interior was decorated with sea pictures. Fish nets hung along the walls beside the pictures. Crab traps were fastened to beams on the ceiling. An upturned canoe formed a counter at the bar.

Tiana selected a table beside windows at the back of the room. These windows provided a view of a pond, or widening of a stream, where an heron stalked the shallow water. After Tiana sat down on a chair on one side of the table, Ronald sat at the opposite side. A waitress arrived. She had long, brown hair tied at the back and her eyes were also brown. She was an attractive woman who appeared to be an hard working person who didn't bother with unnecessary conversation. She lit a candle located at the center of the table. When a flickering flame cast golden light across Tiana's attractive face and pale blue eyes, Ron said to himself, I'm not going to think about anything. I'm just going to enjoy this situation.

"Oysters?" asked the waitress.

"Yes, thanks," replied Tiana.

"They're an house specialty," added the waitress. "We get them from Malpec Bay in Prince Edward Island."

The waitress provided menus then said, "Anything to drink?"

"Draft please," answered Tiana.

"The same, thanks," added Ron.

The waitress walked away and Ronald said to Tiana, "You do this every day?"

"Just when I have important things to check with a person," she replied. "You're Ronald Shellton and you own a section of land, east of town, called Spirit Swamp?"

"That's right," he said as the waitress placed a platter of shucked oysters on the table. She walked away and returned to put two, large mugs of beer beside the platter.

"Ready to order?" she asked.

"Fish sandwich," said Tiana.

"The same," added Ron.

"Okay," replied the waitress before she walked toward the counter where she sent the orders to a cook in the kitchen.

After Ron and Tia had placed vinegar and salt on oysters then swallowed two each, and followed them with drinks of beer, Tia said, "I work for a nonprofit, environmental, protection company. We purchase land to protect it and save it in a natural state as a refuge for wildlife. We would like to buy Spirit Swamp."

"I'm not interested in selling it because I work there," answered Ron while he added vinegar to another oyster. "I'm not going to do anything else with the land. Therefore you don't have to worry about it. I'm going to leave the swamp just as it is. It's a beautiful place for painting and I'm going to leave it as a refuge."

"That's good," said Tia after she downed another oyster. She drank more beer.

The waitress placed plates of steaming food on the table. Aromas were tantalizing and indicated good cooking.

"Thanks," said Tiana to the waitress.

"Will this be on one bill or two?" the waitress asked Ron.

"One," replied Tia.

The waitress walked toward other customers as both Ron and Tia added sauce along with vinegar, salt and pepper to the food.

"If you decide to sell the swamp, will you only sell to us?" asked Tia before she gave Ron a card containing, in bold letters, the name and address of the Environmental Protection Society.

"I agree to only sell to this company if I decide to sell," said Ron.

"Thanks," replied Tiana. She was finding him to be easy to talk with and his company seemed natural.

Watching her in light from the flame, Ron thought, she's very attractive and I get along with her easily. She seems to be full of surprises. I'm just going to enjoy this situation and not think about everything.

"There's something else I wanted to ask you," continued Tia as she used her knife and fork to neatly cut a steaming chunk of fish. "I'm an archaeologist. I've heard about the legends regarding Spirit Swamp. I was wondering if I could have your permission to do some archaeological work in the swamp? This would involve some digs and other exploratory research of the area."

"Would any damage be done to the swamp?" asked Ronald. "This fish is delicious by the way."

"Yes," said Tiana. "I don't come here often although I know it's a good restaurant. The beer's good too."

"Beer usually is good," said Ron.

"No damage would be done to the land," she added. "I'm an environmentalist and won't do any harm to the swamp."

"Are you talking about a large operation with bulldozers and stuff?" he asked.

"No," she answered. "The work would be small and limited without doing any damage."

"Are many people involved?" he asked.

"No," she said. "There would be just myself and a few others. Since you work there also, you would be able to check what was being done on your property."

"Your request sounds sensible," said Ron. "I can't see any reason why you shouldn't be doing some excavating along with investigating."

"I'm relieved to hear you say that," she exclaimed.

"More beer?" asked the waitress who had approached unnoticed.

"Yes, thanks," replied Tiana. Turning again to Ron, Tiana said, "I didn't think you would mind if I worked in the swamp. However, I couldn't be sure of anything until I actually got your permission."

"You have my approval to work in the swamp," said Ron. "Where would you be working?"

"At the spring mostly," she replied. "The spring used to be much larger in earlier times. More water emerged from the ground, making a large pond. Now the spring has almost dried up and the surrounding clay-filled earth could be easily excavated. The spring should show a cross section of life from mammoths to the present time.

Indian nations have used the swamp and there have also been other fur trappers and settlers along with loggers."

"You seem to already know much about the swamp," observed Ron.

"I walk through there all the time," she replied.

"You should visit my camp," said Ron. "I have a tent camp in the woods southeast of the spring."

"I've seen your tents," she said. "No one has been in the camp any time I walked there."

"I haven't been there often," said Ron. "I'm planning to live in the swamp and do my paintings in my camp."

"I should see you the next time I'm walking in the woods," said Tiana.

Ronald was aware of how much he was enjoying this woman's company. It's like she has cast some sort of a spell around here and I'm enjoying her presence, he thought.

Tiana said to herself, this supper has gone better than I could have possibly expected. I enjoy this guy's company naturally. I'm lucky this time and I've never been lucky before with men.

The waitress was handing Ron the bill when Tiana gave her some money. Taking the payment, the waitress said, "I'll get your change."

"I would appreciate paying the bill because I have enjoyed this whole thing," said Ron.

"There's not much sense in paying the bill twice," she replied.

The waitress returned and placed change on the table. Tiana left the money for the tip.

"Thanks," said Ron.

"I suppose we should leave," said Tia as she stood up.

Standing also, Ron said, "Thanks for supper."

"I'll tell my helpers that we can start checking the swamp," added Tia while they walked to the doorway. They stepped outside among shadows of evening.

"I'll see you in the swamp," she said before turning and walking toward a green van.

Ron went to a grocery store. After purchasing some supplies, he took them to his van. He felt elated about something and wasn't quite sure what it was until he realized he was particularly happy because of his meeting with Tiana

Benton. She's naturally pleasing to me, he reflected. Everything seems right. I'm in a good mood that's sort o' like a fine intoxication. Maybe these good spells occur when life lines up correctly. I'm just going to enjoy this situation and not think too much.

Having placed the packages in the back of his van, he opened the driver's door and sat on the seat. He closed the door, started the motor and said to himself, I enjoyed the supper and I'm usually not inclined to like such things.

I'll return to my camp and do some painting, he thought as he left the parking lot and started driving along the road. Summer is a particularly beautiful time of year with deep, green colors in the landscape.

Ron drove onto the lane and parked his van. Having unpacked his supplies, he started walking along remnants of the tote road. The sun had set and there remained sufficient light to identify the outlines of the road, or trail, through the woods. I had to use the trail because there isn't sufficient light for me to walk directly through the swamp, Ron said to himself. The loggers who started this route followed the available, high terrain winding between all the ponds.

Upon approaching the vicinity of his camp, Ronald turned away from the trail and walked along a ridge between two ponds. I almost don't have sufficient light to determine where I'm going. I could get lost in here although, fortunately, I can now see my tents.

He was relieved to reach his camp. It consisted of three tents. His main tent was situated on a crest of land surrounded by hemlocks and facing a pond. This pond connected with the water at the spring and all the swamp's water drained northward into Spring Creek that flowed to Willow River. None of the ponds were large although they were part of more extensive, wet or swampy sections.

Next to the main, painting tent, there was a cook tent. Its pump took water from the pond and also supplied water to an attached shower tent. The cook tent contained food supplies along with a stove heated by propane. All food was locked in secure containers. An outhouse was located among a dense stand of hemlocks and cedars to the southwest.

Well, I'm home, Ron said to himself after he had turned on some propane lights. He collected kindling then started a fire on top of ashes in front of the main tent. This structure contained a cot in addition to painting facilities.

Having prepared tea, he sat down on his favorite chair in front of the main tent. The area was protected by a tarp stretching from the top of the tent to the edge of the fireplace.

This camp isn't permanent, he noted. Everything could be removed easily. Maybe someday I'll build an art studio. I like the protective wall of hemlocks. There are also numerous birches and beeches. The scenery here is as wild and beautiful as any I've seen. Raccoons visit sometimes although I don't have anything they are able to damage. Most of the animals and birds of the region live in this forest. Fortunately I don't often see bear tracks.

Ron added extra wood to the fire. Afterward, he refilled his cup with steaming, green tea and sat down again in front of the warming fire. Its light flickered across hemlock trunks and branches. Jumping light also illuminated a gray birch. Stars were scattered across a patch of sky that was visible between the tarp and trees. An owl hooted from the swamp in the northeast. Leopard frogs croaked occasionally. From high terrain, to the north, a wolf howled. Resembling a wisp of drifting smoke, a fox passed along the far side of the pond. The animal walked steadily, checking the water's edge. The rounded form of a raccoon moved down a tree's trunk and quickly became lost from view among shadows. A flying squirrel dropped onto the trunk of the birch next to camp then scurried up this trunk.

There's much to see in the forest if I just sit down and watch rather than stir around and disturb everything, observed Ron. A campfire doesn't seem to worry the critters.

When Ron became too tired to enjoy watching the woods, he went to his cot and slept until, at daybreak, he heard geese honking. Ducks could be heard quacking on a distant pond.

Having prepared a breakfast of bacon, eggs, toast and coffee, he decided to walk along his main trail. He proceeded northward until he could see water at the spring. He turned eastward, following high ground containing willows and maples. Ponds were north and south of this elevated section. The land became flatter then he saw the remnants of the cabin. He continued eastward and stepped along the trunk of a fallen tree stretching across a narrow section of a pond. Beyond this narrow section, the forest became particularly dense with both brush and trees. The earth was low and damp. Porcupines had been chewing on a few trees. Hearing tapping sounds, Ron looked to his side in time to see an herd of deer bounding out of view.

He walked along the edge of bulrushes in a vast, watery area before he came again to high land containing numerous birches and maples. Continuing onward, each step brought him to a changed view of the wild and endlessly beautiful swamp. With a booming of wings, ruffed grouse took to flight and flew to a section of hemlocks. Ron saw turkeys moving in a line and stepping quickly out of sight.

Ron walked to a trail that had earlier been a tote road. Leaving this route, he checked the site of the old, logging camp. Two doors remained hinged to tree trunks. Scattered, ruffed grouse feathers marked the place where a fox had found a meal.

When Ron returned to his camp, he heard noises to the northeast beyond the spring. He walked in this direction until he could see the people near the spring. Farther northward, a trailer and trucks were parked in a line beside the road.

Ron walked toward the spring. Tiana was giving instructions to people next to the water. "Hi," she shouted upon seeing him. "Don't be concerned by the crowd. There's a lot to do just to get started. I'll end up with about three helpers. One of them is over there unloading equipment." Pointing to a woman, Tiana said, "She's Ruth Sloan."

Hearing her name being mentioned, the woman stopped working and walked toward Tiana and Ron. Ruth had black hair tied neatly at the back of her head. She had black eyes and wore a blue, cotton shirt along with jeans and boots. "Hi," she said to Ron, shaking hands with him.

"Ronald Shellton," said Tiana, pointing to him. "He's the one I was telling you about," Tiana added to Ruth. "He's the owner of the property and he is letting us excavate in this area."

"Thanks for helping us," Ruth said to Ron. Her attractive smile revealed even, white teeth. "There're a lot o' stories about this swamp," continued Ruth. "I suppose you've heard most o' them."

"Some of them," replied Ron.

"You're a painter?" asked Ruth.

"Yes," he answered.

"That's your tent camp over there?" she asked, pointing southward.

"Yes," he said.

"We went visiting but nobody has been home," she said.

"I travel around to paint," replied Ron. "You folks can come over any time. I have lots of food and coffee."

"Thanks," said Ruth.

"We are setting up a supply trailer beside the road," said Tia, pointing to the line of trucks and the trailer. "You're welcome to visit also. As I was saying, we have extra help to get started then there will be just a few of us working. Don't let the crowd worry you."

"If you get tired and want some coffee, come over to the tent camp," said Ron.

"Thanks," said Tia.

"Pleased to meet you," added Ruth as Ron started walking back to his camp. The women returned to their work.

Returning to his camp, Ron had a feeling of being pleased with the way his life was proceeding. He had many new paintings he wanted to finish.

During the next weeks, he felt happier than he could remember being previously. Tia visited his camp. He also regularly went to see the workers near the spring and got coffee at the trailer. His paintings were proceeding well. He started to be away from his camp more often to get certain pictures in just the right light.

He had not been introduced to a man at the excavation site although this person was there frequently. This man was large and fat with slicked, grayish-brown hair and moustache along with dark eyes. He didn't seem to do much work although he apparently made the coffee. Coffee was always available at the spring site in addition to the trailer.

One morning, when Ron visited the spring, Ruth was the only worker present. After helping himself to a cup of coffee, he walked over to talk to her. She was using a trowel to remove earth from one of many squared areas beside the spring.

"Doesn't water seep into the holes?" asked Ron.

"Very little water comes out of the spring now," answered Ruth after her trowel scooped out more clay. "The spring was much larger having more water at earlier times. A pond, at one time, covered much of this whole area. During our work, we don't get too close to the flowing water. Therefore we are scraping through dry earth and a lot o' clay."

"Finding anything?" asked Ron.

"A lot o' bones so far," answered Ruth. The bones are from many different kinds of animals. All animals go to a supply of water. Some bones are from mammoths, musk oxen and caribou in addition to the usual moose, deer and wolves."

"You're doing well," exclaimed Ron.

"There's a lot here," said Ruth. She continued to scrape the clay. "We are working carefully and sifting the soil. Most of the bones, of course, are easy to locate especially the mammoth bones."

"Are you doing most of the work?" asked Ron.

"Much of the heavy work has been done," replied Ruth. "Tiana and I are the main workers now."

"Who's the big guy?" asked Ron.

"He's Tiana's boyfriend," she said. "They're getting married. They are going to take a rest and go south to one of the islands, maybe St. Martins. I think they are getting married there. I'm not sure. She doesn't tell me everything." Ruth looked up at Ron and smiled brightly. She thought his face and eyes seemed paler than usual.

"Oh, I see," he said as calmly as possible. "She doesn't tell me everything either. You're working well. I guess I should also get busy."

"Thanks for visiting," said Ruth before Ron started walking toward his camp. The world had become grayer to him although the sun was shining brightly. Strange how I always get the wrong slant on things, he told himself. My world just collapsed when she said, "He's Tiana's boyfriend."

Ronald was in a state of shock. He couldn't work and found little interest in going for walks.

He had just finished breakfast when he saw three men approaching from the south. They've come from the tote road trail, thought Ron. That's unusual. Why would they be on the trail? Maybe that was a motor I heard earlier coming from the south. I wonder what they're doing.

The man walking in front of the other two was the large guy from the excavation site. He was the person Ruth identified as Tiana's boyfriend.

"Hi," the large man shouted roughly.

Ron did not answer. These men were trespassing and Ron felt cold although the morning was warm.

"You Ron Shellton?" demanded a second man.

"Could be," said Ron. "What are you doin' here?"

"We came to tell you to stay away from Tiana Benton," said the big guy.

"What business could that be of yours?" replied Ron.

"That's my business," stated the fat man. He pointed to one man and this person walked eastward. The fat man pointed at the third man and he stepped westward. Ron picked up his axe. The other men pulled short clubs from their jackets.

"We're just goin' for a ride so you'll stay away from Tia," stated the fat man.

Stepping toward the large guy, Ron thought, he's the leader. If I get him, the others will leave.

Ron heard boots tapping against the ground, coming toward him from both sides. He turned one way and got hit on the head from the opposite direction. A light flashed and he lost consciousness.

NINE

THE VISION

Ronald Shellton regained consciousness occasionally. Each time he was awake, the bright sunlight increased a flashing pain in his head. When the night came with stars in a murky sky, he tried to remain conscious although his head ached. There was a sharp pain in his side along with his leg and all of these searing aches seemed to fuse together into such excruciating pain he felt a rushing sound in his head.

He touched lumps on his head. Although there were no bumps on his side, he was certain that the sharp pains indicated he had at least one broken rib. His leg sent a chilling trickle of fear coursing through him. The leg bone bulged against the skin between the knee and ankle.

Knowing what he had to do, he used his hands to lift the foot of his injured leg. Having wedged this foot into the fork in a trunk of a small tree, he lurched backwards, forcing the broken bone to slip back into place with a clunking sound. He screamed with the pain and slumped   backwards,   losing consciousness.

Much later, when he opened his eyes, the sunlight jolted his headache. His entire body seemed to be wracked by severe pain. Sudden movements sent sharp pains stabbing into his side.

Noticing his painting pack beside him, he checked its contents, hoping to find his knife. He emptied the pack and there was no knife.

Using both hands to hold his injured leg, he carefully lifted it out of the fork in the tree's trunk. He broke saplings to make splints. By ripping one sleeve of his shirt, he got ties to secure the splints in place against his broken leg.

Small comforts can be great things, he thought before he returned his pipe, matches and cup to the painting bag. I have some essential items in my paint bag.

There's no sign that anyone has walked around here, noted Ron. I must have been lowered, or just dropped, out of an helicopter. They threw my art bag beside me to make my death look like an accident. If any one found me, the police would think I went out painting, as I always do, and just fell then got lost. My easel and boards remain attached to my painting pack. Likely in the rush, no one bothered to open my pack. It seems to be just the way I prepared it. Fortunately, it contains matches in addition to my cup and pipe. Tiana's boyfriend wanted to get rid o' me. He got two of his friends to assist in beating me then dumping me somewhere in a swamp. I'm likely not on my own land; yet I'm probably somewhere in the region. They wouldn't want to kill me too far away from a place I would be painting because the whole thing would have to look like an accident. I'm going to be stranded here for a long time. My ribs, leg and head will have to heal before I can walk very far. There are bulrushes nearby. I can eat these roots. I have matches to start a fire. Fortunately I have my cup along with my pipe and tobacco. Things could be worse.

Ronald rested until his headache subsided. Before I get too weak, I must start moving, he said to himself. I have much to do. There aren't too many black flies or mosquitoes around at this time of the summer. The flies were a problem earlier.

Working slowly to not agitate the soreness in his side, he held a sapling for support and managed to get to a standing position. He hobbled to a fallen maple then broke a forked branch to function as a crutch. Now, at least, I can move around, he thought. With my pack over my back and a crutch to help me walk, I'll search for a camping place with a supply of clean water.

Ronald stepped slowly onward for the remainder of the day. Although the area was wet with large sections of bulrushes, he could not find clean water or high ground for a camp. He rested on the trunk of a fallen willow then slept most of the night.

At daybreak, he resumed traveling. He was becoming increasingly weary as well as thirsty. I must find an excellent site for a camp, he reminded himself. If I can make a comfortable camp, I'll rest until my injuries have healed sufficiently for me to walk out of this swamp. I know I'm not on my own property although I must be somewhat close to Spirit Swamp. If they dropped me too far away from my property, my death would look too much like murder. They tried to injure me so I would die in this swamp. If I can find a good camping place, I'll disappoint the guys who have tried to kill me.

Ron rested then slept through another night. With all this swamp around, there must be clean, running water around somewhere, he thought. I'm going to keep searching while I have enough strength to walk.

He pushed onward until, late in the day, he came to flowing water. It was moving between definite banks. I'll walk upstream and I should find a suitable site, he said to himself. I want high, dry ground and clean water.

Evening shadows were lengthening and darkening throughout the swamp when Ron reached a widening of the stream. A creek splashed into a large pool that had rocky banks. Sloping to the water, high, dry ground was topped by pines and maples along with the numerous willows. This is a perfect place for my recuperation, Ron exclaimed to himself as he stepped onto a grassy bank overlooking a stream splashing into the pool. Much of the rock here is flint, he observed. Broken pieces of flint are scattered in piles mixed with hammer stones. The Indian people have come here to get flint. I could use fragments to function as knives or axe heads. I'll also make arrows and spears so I can hunt for food. I must work slowly and let my broken bones heal without any setbacks.

Ronald selected chunks of flint to be employed as knives or larger cutting tools. With such equipment, he first cut a more comfortable crutch. Next he removed boughs to make a mattress. Upon completing the mattress, he stretched out on the scented, cushion and slept for the remainder of the night.

At dawn, Ron started building a lean-to. He worked slowly and built a solid structure shingled with overlapping boughs. In front of his new home, he used flat stones to construct a fireplace.

Although he was weary and hungry, he enjoyed the wild beauty of the landscape. He rested in his shelter and watched the fire in front of the pond. Its calm surface reflected the surrounding swamp. An heron occasionally stalked shallow water beside the far bank. Leopard frogs croaked from the pond. Other croaking sounds could be heard from innumerable places in the swamp. Sometimes a clear call of a whippoorwill rang through the night. The forest, at night, was alive with splashing sounds in addition to honking cries of geese and the quacking chatter of ducks. When a chorus of bullfrogs added deeper voices to swamp noises, Ronald said to himself, I think I hear supper calling.

He picked up a stick he had selected to use as a skewer. Armed with this makeshift spear, he stepped into shallow water. He had learned to use the crutch skillfully and found he could move around most obstacles.

Ron could see the bullfrogs protruding above the water's surface. When he threw his spear, it missed its target. Targets were numerous, however, and he soon speared a large frog. He held this frog then speared another and took them to camp.

Using flint chips as knives, Ron prepared the legs and skewered them on a stick above the flames. In a short time, the meat cooked. He found the meat to be juicy and delicious. These legs are much like small chicken legs, noted Ron after savoring the food.

He slept well during the night, getting up occasionally to add wood to the fire. In the morning, he went hunting for more frogs. He collected many clams in addition to bulrush roots and water cress. He also collected immature grains of wild rice.

There's actually lots o' food around here, he said to himself before enjoying a meal of frog legs roasted on a skewer accompanied by clams and roots cooked in hot ashes. Now that I have food and shelter along with clean water, I'm going to make a bow and arrows together with some spears. Improved weapons will enable me to hunt for ruffed grouse, turkeys and deer.

He was collecting wood for the construction of a bow in addition to arrows and spears when he noticed a patch of fine sand littered by remnants of turtle eggs. Protruding from this sand, there was a section of a pottery bowl. He scooped away adjacent sand and carefully removed the bowl. It was a beautifully shaped, pottery pot with lines and dots incised in the clay. I can use this pot to make soup and tea, Ron exclaimed to himself.

He carried the bowl to his shelter then returned to get the wood he had selected to fashion weapons. Cord removed from his jacket would serve as a bowstring. He used pieces of flint to cut and shape a bow. He hardened the wood by holding it over the fire.

Having constructed a fine bow, he carved some spears along with numerous, arrow shafts. With each arrow's shaft, he cut a notch in one end. In the opposite end, he cut short splits for the insertion of flint points. He feathered each arrow by removing thread from his jacket and using this thread to tie split feathers in place. He also secured these feathers using heated pine pitch.

When all other work had been completed, he started the task of chipping flint arrowheads, spear points and knives. He quickly discovered that he had a natural skill for chipping flint. He worked in sunlight in front of his shelter. At night he continued each task, chipping flints almost with a feverish interest. The fire created warmth in addition to providing suitable, although flickering light. He kept busy during each night and day. Added to times for necessary sleep, he took breaks in order to rest while he sipped tea made from immature, wild rice. His clam chowder simmered in the bowl and provided a delicious meal.

Ron was fascinated by the enjoyment he found in making use of his natural skill for fashioning points and knives from flint. After finishing his initial work, he wasn't able to leave the pieces undecorated. On each arrowhead, spear point or knife, he employed a particularly sharp chip of flint to scratch beautiful drawings of standing bears.

I'm in a different time, he told himself. I've gone back in time. I'm beyond being an Indian hunter. I think I've entered the realm of a prehistoric hunter. I have made flint-tipped spears and arrows together with two, flint knives. Each object I make out of flint contains a beautifully etched bear. I enjoy this work and am amazed by the fine shape of each piece along with the beautifully accurate drawings of bears. I like to—almost feel compelled to—etch a standing bear on each arrowhead. That's my mark or my signature. I feel more at home—or as much at home—in this way of life as I was in the more modern life.

I made the weapons in order to hunt for extra food, reflected Ron after he had prepared more rice tea. He sat down again, sipped the tea, and thought, this tea is a refreshing treat. I also like the stew I've been making. Maybe I'll just continue using the food I already have and I won't shoot any other critters. I don't want to hurt anything unnecessarily. I just have to get enough food for my survival. I'm doing well with a diet of roots, water cress, clams and frogs.

Days passed, joining into weeks and becoming months. During this time, Ronald's injuries healed. He adapted completely to life in the swamp. He bathed in the pond and also washed his clothes by making a soap substitute through combining ashes and sand. His cooking improved, enabling him to make a variety of meals using the usual clams, frogs, roots and water cress.

He had become strong again and ready to leave camp. Fear trickled coldly across his skin when he saw the huge tracks on top of his own boot prints along a muddy section of the swamp. Those are bear tracks, he told himself. They aren't ordinary, bear tracks because these deep, large prints have been made by a grizzly and this hunter is following me. There are a few grizzlies around in some connecting, wilderness areas. I'm in an isolated place and maybe an ideal location for anything that is wild. I can't ignore such tracks. I must have my spears and arrows ready for action. Possibly I could trap, or snare, this creature before it catches me.

Ronald sensed the presence of something ominous when he detected a musty scent drifting in air currents. Being aware of some kind of a presence before hearing the grunt, he turned around in time to see the grizzly walking toward him. The hump-backed bear kept advancing with massive muscles moving under thick fur. A breeze rippled this same fur. Hoping the approaching terror was just a dream, Ronald, at the same time, knew the animal was real and was coming to kill in much the same chilling way a cat comes to kill a bird.

Ronald fitted an arrow to the string on his bow. He pulled back the string and shot the arrow, releasing it too quickly. The shaft whizzed over the great bear's head, sending the creature forward faster.

The second shot sent an arrow cutting into the side of the giant's head. The bear stood up, roaring with rage, and slapped at the shaft, splintering it. The bear resumed its charge until another arrow stuck in the wide chest. The bear slapped at the shaft and drove part of it farther into the body. Cavernous jaws opened and a furious growl spewed out at this enemy that was causing pain.

The bear advanced more cautiously. It was hit on a front leg by another arrow. The shaft pierced the hide and stuck in muscle. However the bear ignored this additional jab of pain and continued walking forward.

An arrow in the throat made the creature stumble. Ronald took this downward movement as a chance to advance. He sprang passed the bear and shoved a spear into the side of the creature. The bear swung around and tried to sink teeth into Ronald's leg. Ronald stepped away from this thrust before forcing a second spear into the giant's throat. The bear opened large jaws and came forward as Ron tried to move out of the way and fell backward. The jaws came down toward Ron's head. Blood flowed from the mouth. The grizzly's breath stank of fish. The bear fell on Ronald who thought he saw death coming. However, with disbelief and joyous thankfulness for being alive, he realized that the bear was dead.

Ronald pulled himself out from under the furred and heavy form. He trembled almost uncontrollably. He stopped shaking gradually. Working slowly, he retrieved his weapons, saving the flint points and discarding the broken shafts.

After returning to his camp, he stretched out in the stream, allowing its water to flow around him and soothe his nerves. I've enjoyed my life in this swamp, he thought. I'm sorry the bear died but I was not ready to be killed. I'm going to collect my weapons, paint bag and pottery bowl then I'll return to Spirit Swamp.

Ronald was weary yet, following his escape from the bear, he was appreciating the enjoyment of being alive. When he was sleeping, he saw himself in a vision. He was an hunter, carrying a bow and arrow together with spears and a pottery bowl. He walked to Spirit Swamp and visited the spring where he met his wife who was called Shell. "Arrowmaker," she exclaimed. "It's time you returned and you brought my bowl."

"Shell," he replied. "It's time you returned and you have my arrow and spear points. I was never away."

Daniel Hance Page

TEN

THE RETURN

Ronald woke up when he heard wolves howling in the north. He collected his weapons and placed the bowl along with other possessions in the art bag. He started walking with his back to the rising sun. He walked slowly yet steadily, being careful with his leg.

When night came, he slept while resting his back against a willow trunk. In the morning, he walked until he was facing the sun. He came upon a road and thought he recognized it. He walked along this road and, in a short time, he could identify all of his surroundings. Proceeding onward, he reached another road. It followed it until he saw the trailer.

Evening was approaching when he passed the trailer and walked toward the spring. A woman was working beside the spring. He recognized Tiana Benton. She stood up, walked to a fence post, got a rifle and waited.

The man kept approaching. Tiana held the rifle, pointing its barrel to the ground. Sometimes I

don't like working out here alone,
she thought. This man looks wild.
I'll shoot if I have to protect
myself.

The man had wind-swept hair and
a beard. His clothes were torn
although they seemed to be clean.
He carried a pack and a bow along
with arrows and spears.

Approaching her, he held the
bowl out to her. Thinking the
offered bowl might be a trick to get
her to put down the gun, she waited.
"You don't recognize me?" he asked
incredulously.

"You're not Ronald Shellton?"
she asked looking pale.

"Yes, of course," he exclaimed.
Stepping forward, she gave him a
bear hug while he continued holding
the bowl.

She stepped back, saying, "The
bowl is for me?"

"Yes," he replied.

She took the bowl. Holding it
carefully in her hands, she asked,
"What has happened to you?" She
continued to be shocked by his
appearance.

"That's a long story," he
answered.

"Where did you get the bow,
arrows and spears?" she asked,

taking a spear and staring at its point.

"I made them," he said.

"They're ancient," she exclaimed.

"Then I made them in an ancient way," he answered.

"Who put the bears on them?" she asked.

"I did," he replied.

"You're joking," she said.

"I drew the bears on each flint piece I made," he countered.

"Did you come here and get our arrowheads and spear points?" she asked.

"No," he said, not knowing why she was obsessed with the flint points. "I didn't know you were so interested in arrowheads and spearheads."

"Well look at the points I found beside the spring," she said, removing points from her jacket pocket. She held them beside the points Ronald had made and they were the same. She stared at him in disbelief. "You don't believe you were here a long time ago?" she said softly.

"That's your bowl," he replied.

"Thanks for giving it to me," she answered.

231

"It's yours because you made it," he said.

"Yeah, sure," she gasped. "Some things I don't understand."

"I don't know everything either," he replied. "I saw you, though, in a vision and, according to this vision, we met a long time ago. If people live forever, what do you think they do? Do they come back?" She seemed shocked by his questions, so he asked, "What else did you find during your checking of this area?"

"We have uncovered amazing things," she replied. "We've found bones. There are a lot o' animal bones such as those belonging to a mammoth, musk ox, caribou and wolf. We found human bones. They're very old. We got some bear tooth pendants. They have standing bears etched on them. A lot of flint points are also marked by etchings of standing bears. A shell amulet looks like a wolf. We found stone thunderbirds and a pottery bowl along with other shards and effigy pipes. In the cabin, we uncovered a journal written by Jasper Ridge." She stopped talking, stared at him then asked, "What happened to you?"

"Your friend, the big guy, tried to kill me," said Ron. "The big guy, along with two friends, gave me a severe beating then dumped me in a swamp, intending that I would die and the whole thing would look like an accident caused by my wanderings as an artist. I recovered and came back. Did you get married?"

"No," she said. "There was someone else."

"Someone else?" he asked.

"You," she said. "It is time you returned and you brought my bowl."

"It is time you returned," he said, "and you have my arrow and spear points. I was never away."

"Where are we going to live?" she asked.

"We can build a permanent house and studio over at my camp," he replied. "I'll continue painting the swamp and you can write its story."

ABOUT THE AUTHOR

Daniel Hance Page is a freelance writer, specialized in environmental and North American Indian issues, with eight previous books published and numerous others being written. His books depict the history and culture of the United States and Canada with authentic stories that are filled with spiritual insight along with action, adventure, history and travel.